RACE AND ROMANCE
Coloring the Past

by
MARGO HENDRICKS

Arizona Center
for Medieval and
Renaissance Studies
ACMRS PRESS
Arizona State University
Tempe, Arizona
2022

ACMRS PRESS

Race and Romance: Coloring the Past was published in 2022 by ACMRS Press at Arizona State University in Tempe, Arizona.
Licensed under a Creative Commons Attribution-NonCommercial 4.0 International License, except where otherwise noted.

This book is available online at https://asu.pressbooks.pub/race-and-romance/

Library of Congress Cataloging-in-Publication Data
Librarians will find the cataloging data for this book online. It was not available at the time of this printing.(LCCN: 2022008523)

Hardcover ISBN 978-0-86698-694-6
Paperback ISBN 978-0-86698-659-5
eISBN 978-0-86698-695-3

Hardcover and paperback editions are printed in the United States of America.

Contents

Dear Reader   vii

Introduction   xi

Chapter One   1
Debating the Obvious

Chapter Two   15
So Like Her Father

Chapter Three   35
Settling an Isle, or and Englishman's Color

Chapter Four   55
Seeing What You Want

Chapter Five   73
Looking and Seeing

Chapter Six   89
"Fictions of the Pose": Act I, Scene 2

Epilogue   103

Works Cited   107

Dear Reader,

The skeletal remains of this little book lay untouched for a decade on my computer. Like the ghostly memories of the personal and social histories that brought me to the academy, this manuscript hovered at the edges of my awareness and on my desktop for over a decade, at times a visceral reminder of the tyranny white supremacy can and does wield so thoroughly on Black, Brown, Asian, and Indigenous minds and bodies. The manuscript has resurfaced. Its scriptoral body marginally repaired with trembling muscles and a faintly beating heart because there are academic peers and friends who believed I had silenced my scholar's voice long enough. In its original version, *Race and Romance: Coloring the Past* was nearly three hundred pages excluding notes – the type of monograph expected of someone seeking promotion to full professor. This is not that book, although it stands in fulfillment of a promise made. This is a messy book because of the personal and non-personal events that made it difficult to complete: white supremacy, COVID-19, the deaths of two siblings, the loss of hundreds of thousands of lives in the United States because of one white man's narcissism, and, because it bears repeating, white supremacy. That *Race and Romance* came into existence amid all of this is a testament to the weight of a promise.

During the writing and re-writing of this book, I chose to shed the coat of "citational authority." In the original manuscript, Chapter One had over eighty footnotes, a third were explanatory or served as justifications for assertions made in my analysis. In my first effort to "revise" the original manuscript, I left these discursive and citational footnotes intact. I also stopped working on the manuscript for a while. Once a draft was completed, I understood why I stopped. When I took on emerita status, I embraced the actual mode of writing I always wanted to do, romance fiction. Scholarly writing took away from that, even though my academic research feeds the world-building I undertake in my romance novels. Once I embarked on fiction writing, I realized that for much of my career in higher education I had held myself to a presumed standard of perfectionism that many white academics simply do not adhere to, or at least not in the same way.

At the time I entered the profession as a "Renaissance English Literature and Shakespearean" scholar, the number of Black Americans at the assistant professor level at R1 institutions was tiny. I recall walking into my first Shakespeare Association of America annual conference, and feeling a sense of relief when I spied two or three dark-skinned faces among the hundreds of white Shakespeareans in the room. With each successive conference, this scenario never really changed despite a small yet steady increase in the number of Black, Indigenous, Brown, and People of Color who embarked on the study of Shakespeare or early modern English culture. Even so, there is the struggle to publish, to have your scholarship respected or even acknowledged, to have your identity recognized (I will forever be Kim Hall as she will be me as I will be Joyce Green MacDonald as she will be me as Ayanna Thompson will be me as she will be Kim Hall). The lessons I learned from a number of my white Shakespeare and early modern peers is that you don't see me as the person and subject Margo Hendricks; rather, I am one of a half dozen Black Shakespeareans who move among you unrecognizable as individual subjects not because of a political humanist belief in equality but because white supremacy are the glasses you wear and refuse to remove. What this experience taught me was that "looking" and "seeing" are two quite different epistemological operations.

It is the combined practice of looking and seeing that informs the narrative of *Race and Romance: Coloring the Past*. Except for Beverly Jenkins's *Forbidden* and *Indigo*, all of the literary texts subject to my musing are early modern romances and ones that appear to center white characters. *Appear*, of course, being the operative term. What you can expect in reading this book is a set of musings on colorism and racism, on white passing and white presenting, on the romance genre, on Aphra Behn and Black romance author Beverly Jenkins, on Heliodorus's *Aethiopica* and its literary descendants. This is a book I wanted to write in 2008 but couldn't because I didn't fully grasp the insidiousness of academic white supremacy until I retired. There will be critiques; some readers wishing I had gone deeper into analysis, others that I had played the "scholar's part." There are areas where I could perhaps have done far more citational homage but I do not have to write a book or article to maintain my status as an emerita professor. I also firmly believe that the generation of premodern critical race studies and critical indigenous studies scholars currently shaping the field have so much to teach me and others, I should not get in their way.

Finally, I am not certain this book would exist in its present form or even written had I not retired. However, without gentle nudges from Kim F. Hall, Ayanna Thompson, Arthur Little, Ambereen Dadabhoy, and Lehua Kim, I would be sitting comfortably agonizing over writing paranormal, historical, and contemporary romance novels that center Black women's happily ever afters. Instead, I thank these amazing friends, the Folger Library, *RaceB4Race*, and ACMRS Press, especially Roy Ruklia and Geoffrey Way, for their encouragement. Whatever is problematic about this book is on me as this is the only single-author academic book I will write.

Introduction

> Disciplinary knowledge, then, is more than the sum of separate
> inquiries in discrete areas of knowledge. It is part of a historically
> specific body of knowledge, an episteme, that contains premises,
> presumptions, and practices that work together to hide the
> workings of racialized power.
>
> (Crenshaw et al. 2019, 11)

When I began my research and publication activity in what was called
Renaissance English literature (this includes Willie Shakespeare), my
efforts to argue colorism and racial taxonomies were not anomalies but
very much part of early modern English cultural and political ideologies
were seen as anachronistic. Race and racism were viewed as products
of nineteenth-century scientific and imperialist discourse. From the lofty
seat of hindsight, I now realize I was working to articulate the process of
racecraft in early modern English culture.

According to Barbara J. Fields and Karen E. Fields, *race, racism,* and
racecraft are distinctive. *Race* is rooted in the idea of biophysical differences among groups while *racism* is the social practice or "action" taken
based on the idea of race. In other words, "*race* is the principal unit and
core concept of *racism*" (Fields and Fields 2014, 17). *Racecraft*, on the other
hand, "originates not in nature but in human action and imagination; it
can exist in no other way. The action and imagining are collective yet individual, day-to-day yet historical, and consequential even though nested in
mundane routine" (17). Importantly, Fields and Fields contend, "*racecraft* is
not a euphemistic substitute for racism. It is a kind of fingerprint evidence
that racism has been on the scene" (17). What is obvious is we cannot have
one without the other but, and this is an important caveat, without racism
there is no race or racecraft.

Fields and Fields's assertion about the relationship between racism and
race reiterates the the arguments put forth in Stuart Hall's and Paul
Gilroy's writings on racism and English colonialism. In "Race the Floating
Signifier: What More Is There to Say about 'Race,'" Stuart Hall reminds us
(citing W.E.B. Du Bois), "color, though of little meaning in itself, is really

important ... 'as a badge for the social heritage of slavery, the dissemina-
tion and the insult of that experience.' A badge, a token, a sign: here indeed
is the idea ... that race is a signifier, and that racialized behavior and difference needs to be understood as a discursive, not necessarily as a genetic
or biological fact" (Hall 2021, 361). Yet, as both Du Bois and Hall grasped,
dismantling the racecraft that insists we start from colorism is not an easy
task. Anglo-American racial capitalism sustains itself on a false dichotomy
of colorism, which in turn feeds the anti-Blackness so pervasive in contemporary Anglo-American cultures. In essence, as Gilroy observes, "in
the way that modern racism works, blackness is the body and whiteness
is the mind, you know the way those Manichean pairings, those dualistic
couples are organised" (Gilroy et al. 2019, 6).

Romance and Racecraft

Race and Romance: Coloring the Past is an exploration of two genres, *race*,
which is grasped as rooted in nature and marked by biophysical traits
(principally color), and *romance*, a category of fiction-writing with specific aims and properties. What link these genres in my view are discursive practices or conventions that shape their cultural intelligibilty, and it
is this "intelligibility," or understanding, that intrigues me. Two questions
center the discussion in this book: How do we recognize race as the prod-
uct of racism, and not the reverse? And, how do we reach an understanding of romance contributions to racism and white supremacy? I aim to
address, if not answer, these questions through an exploration of the ways
the romance genre helps to transform "racism into race, leaving black
persons in view while removing white persons from the stage" (Fields
and Fields 2014, 28). My previous publications explored questions of race-
making as an "already in play" ideology. This book is a departure as it
attends more carefully to the racecraft at work in early modern romances.
Specifically, I examine the "fingerprints" of sixteenth- and seventeenth-
century English racism, attenuated in colorism and anxiety about whiteness and white passing in romance fiction.
   Why make colorism the focus of this book the gentle reader might ask?
Isn't romance a genre that celebrates love, despite all obstacles, and happily ever afters? The answer, dear reader, is in the question. Because the

romance genre trades in happily ever afters and love, it is easy to overlook its participation in the formation of early modern English white suprema- cist logic. By the time non-white romance authors became an active pres- ence within the romance industry, romance and whiteness had become nearly synonymous in the arena of love. What attention to the racecraft at work in the writing of romance fiction generates is a portrait of colorism and negation. What I hope to illustrate is beginning with the transla- tion and circulation of Heliodorus's*Aethiopica*, circa mid-sixteenth cen- tury, the romance genre, the idea of "romance," and colorism have long been intertwined in subtle and not-so-subtle ways. Yet, with a few recent exceptions, to read scholarship on the subject, one would assume other- wise. Some of the blame may be laid at the doorstep of "romance is not literary" claims that routinely surface in critical debates.

What, then, are we to make of pre- and early modern romance "novels" such as *Aethiopica*, or Mary Wroth's *Urania*, or Philip Sidney's *Arcadia*, or odd little novellas such as Henry Neville's *Isle of the Pines*, or the "nov- els" of the "ingenious" Aphra Behn? Do we ignore the occasional "silliness" of plots or storylines and focus on the complexities of the world-building and lyrical prose so that these texts fall out of the category "romance nov- els" into the cauldron of Literature? Why are these pre- and early mod- ern "romance" novels *literary* and the romance novels of Beverly Jenkins, Sarah Maclean, Lisa Kleypas, Courtney Milan, or Alyssa Cole (and many others) classified as *genre or popular fiction* and thus outside the para- meters of Literature? In other words, what is the constitutive difference among these authors even though their fiction adheres to the generic conventions of romance?

Race and Romance: Coloring the Past refuses to engage the question *is romance literary?* I have no interest in playing the problematic "canoncity" game. This book takes as a given that the romance genre is a literary form and one of the oldest literatures. Despite the centuries-long debates about romance (romance versus history, romance versus epic, or finally, romance versus literary fiction), the genre remains the most popular form of literature in the twenty-first century. Rather than treat the literary legitimacy of the genre, I examine the interplay of racism and romance in service of modern white supremacy. Since the late sixteenth century, English language romance as a literary genre and a cultural ideology has been projected through a lens of whiteness, heterosexuality, patriarchal-ism, and class consciousness. This projection generated a range of complicated social and cultural relationships between romance readers and the genre that remain in place. Although there has been a shift in romance authorship from primarily white writers to a more heterogenous group, especially in the United States, colorism retains its hold on the romance publishing industry.

In large measure this stranglehold can be traced in the tangled web of literary historiography, racism, and publishing practices that marks not just the emergence of the "modern" romance novel but also the service to which the genre has been put in support of racial capitalism. According to Nancy Leong, racial capitalism is described as "deriving social or economic value from the racial identity of another person" (Leong 2013, 2152). In particular, racial capitalism is the process "in which a white individual or a predominately white institution derives social or economic value from associating with individuals with nonwhite racial identities" (2154). Because racial capitalism is also a "systemic phenomenon" (2152) in which "nonwhiteness has … become something desirable[,] for many, it has become a commodity to be pursued, captured, possessed, and used" (2155).

Race and Romance: Coloring the Past makes a claim for seeing colorism as a commodity, and in particular the performative subject positions of white passing and white presenting depicted as as simultaneously valu-able and unprofitable in romance fiction. Throughout this book, I make a distinction between white-passing and white-presenting Black peoples. While whiteness is key to both descriptors, *white passing* is the choice to act on the appearance of white presenting for social, political, and economic advantage. Of the practice, Allyson Hobbs writes,

> "passing" is a word that has historically denoted a clandestine and hidden process, designed to leave no trace. Conventional wisdom is that few sources exist because those who passed carefully covered their tracks and left no record of their transgression. The term "passing" suggests a type of instability, a "moving through," or the lack of a stable home or place. Passing was equated both with opportunity (access to white-collar employment, better neighbor-

hoods, a host of social courtesies) and with death (a forever sever-
ing from one's family, friends, and communities). (Hobbs 2018, 134)

Because the *white-passing* individual's color misdirects the observer's
ability to visually locate the passer's racial identity in terms of skin color,
errors and misreadings become functional liabilities and benefits for the
passing subject. Furthermore, both romance and passing are premised on
the fantastic (and seemingly inexplicable) but very real possibility of the
existence of aberrations. It doesn't matter whether the aberrant is localized in mythic fantasy (fairies, dragons, wizards and so on), or in religious
or economic narratives of conquest and settlement, or in the epidermis of
a human being.

White presenting, on the other hand, appears less complicated since
there is no deliberate performance of colorism. The white-presenting
subject may or may not know there are questions about their skin color,
largely because they are perceived as "white," which in turn informs how
they move about the world as a racialized subject. The line between white
presenting and white passing is often blurred but, for the sake of this
book's thematic concerns, I want to hold on to a working distinction
between the two. My discussion treats white presenting as a factor of
social perception rather than a deliberate choice to exploit mispercep-
tion. The white-presenting subject knows or comes to discover their non-
whiteness but that knowledge changes very little about their lives. White
passing is always a performative action in relationship to racism and racial
capitalism. Both subject positions align with the romance genre because
all three are sites of instability. Furthermore, white passing and white presenting expose the idea that we can always perceive the signs of race, and
therefore exist as one of racism's little failures.

As the editors of *Neo-Passing: Performing Identity after Jim Crow* write,
"the aim of the current volume, then, is to understand why passing per-
sists, why it has proliferated, and what might be gained from analyzing its
transformations and unearthing the social, political, and economic conditions that spur on and stem from passing in the late twentieth and into the
twenty-first centuries" (Godfrey and Young 2018, 17). While there has been
a long tradition of scholarly engagement with the act of white passing in
the Americas, particularly the United States, the phenomenon has largely

been ignored in the context of early modern English culture. Centuries of white supremacy and racial capitalism served to refine the racecraft Mollie Godfrey and Vershawn Ashanti Young refer to as "neo-passing" and the white passing/presenting depicted in the romance texts at the center of *Race and Romance*. What is important to both studies is that we conceptualize passing

> as a performance of identity that — once it is described or revealed as passing — provokes conflict rather than cohesion with social expectations or norms, conflicts that might be felt by the passer, various portions of the passer's community, or both. As we argue above, passing is not just a matter of how identities are performed but also a matter of how identity performances are policed. (Godfrey and Young 2018, 12)

What *Race and Romance* seeks to illustrate are the sites of policing and exploitation that mark romance authors' ideological or political engagements with race-based colorism and white-presenting or white-passing subjects. Chapter One offers a summary of the debates on the romance genre and the impact of Heliodorus's romance novel *Aethiopica* on sixteenth- and seventeenth-century English literary culture. I start with Heliodorus's *Aethiopica* because the popularity of this romance novel extended well beyond its Greek origins. Translations, appropriations, and adaptations of the romance of Charikliea and Theagenes kept it present in early modern English culture well beyond Thomas Underdowne's initial translation. Translations and adaptations of *Aethiopica* persisted into the eighteenth century, alongside the continued republication of sixteenth- and seventeenth-centuries works. *Aethiopica* is also one of the earliest romance novels that can legitimately be labeled an interracial romance in the modern sense. Finally, the novel importantly cements both the form (novel) and the idea of romantic relationships in the reader's imagination as expectations of what a romance does.

Chapter Two examines the place of Heliodorus's romance in early modern English racism and racecraft. My focus on two English adaptations of the central plot in *Aethiopica*, the romance of Charikliea and Theagenes, highlights how these adaptations of Heliodorus's *Aethiopica* are used to

ameliorate the racial anxiety associated with the economic and ideological valuation of whiteness within England's settler colonialist and white
supremacy agendas. In this chapter, I look at Edward Fairfax's translation
of Torquato Tasso's *Gerusalem Liberata*, which Fairfax titles *Godfrey of
Bulloigne, or Jerusalem Delivered.* Where Heliodorus offers a happily ever
after ending to his romance novel, the Fairfax/Tasso adaptation does not,
thereby disrupting readerly expectations about the end use of romance
conventions. Crucial to my reading of this adaptation is the slippage that
occurs between white presenting and white passing, and how the early
modern adaptation of *Aethiopica's* storyline prefigures an Anglo-American
preoccupation with whiteness and white supremacy.

In Chapter Three, I turn to Henry Neville's *Isle of Pines.* Normally viewed
as a poltical allegory on Charles II's rule, I argue that Neville's novel is very
much informed by early modern romance genre conventions, plotlines,
and characterizations that would be quite familiar to the text's readership. My reading of the novella through the lens of romance genre and
its conventions examines the racecraft at work in the novel, esepcially
as it relates to English white supremacy and settler colonialism. I argue
that in *Isle of Pines*, the process of race-making reshapes the romance
narrative to align itself with making whiteness visibly invisible. That is,
whiteness becomes percerptible only in relation to the white-presenting
natives born of a Black woman. These "natives" (the Phils) serve as both a
racialized and an indigenous model for white settler colonialist ideologies
of assimilation or genocide. Thus, while the idea of reading *Isle of Pines*
politically is important, this chapter endeavors to reassess the racism and
racecraft coded into the patriarchal ideals in light of romance conventions
embedded in a settler colonialist narrative.

The previous chapters of *Race and Romance* sought to illuminate one
of the most problematic issues in thinking about race, colorism, and
more specifically, white presenting. Prior to the establishment of settler
colonialism and the enslavement of African peoples as part of modern
capitalism, English racism privileged somatic perception when it came
to whiteness and non-whiteness. Translations of Heliodorus's romance
such as Thomas Underdowne's *An Ethiopian History* and William Lisle's
verse rendering, *The Faire Ethiopian*, underplayed the disruptive effects
of white-presenting Africans, while adaptations and borrowings such as

Fairfax/Tasso's *Godfrey of Bulloigne* highlight a growing awareness of the fault lines of racism's use of colorism to code *race* in the service of an ideology of white supremacy. It is these fault lines that Neville's *Isle of Pines* make visible and that the romance novels of Beverly Jenkins and Aphra Behn push to a logical terminus.

In Chapter Four, I argue for seeing Beverly Jenkins's romance novel *Forbidden* as the disruption of the terrain cultivated by the romance texts of Heliodorus, Fairfax/Tasso, Lisle, and Neville. In essence, Jenkins's character Rhine Fontaine is the metamorphosis of the white-presenting figure into the white-passing subject with all its conflicting intersectional social narratives. In Rhine Fontaine, romance meets white supremacy and the logic of white supremacy implodes. Unlike Clorinda or the Phils, Rhine's Blackness and his whiteness may be policed but not erased precisely because it is a performative identity. Jenkins interrogates the colorism that marked not just the enslavement of dark-skinned Africans but also the presumption that whiteness is always white. In Chapters Five and Six, I return to early modern romance fiction with an analysis of Aphra Behn novellas and the specter of a white-passing authorial subjectivity. In particular, I read Behn's novellas as both exempla of white-passing romances *and* as an excavation of a racially performative identity by the novellas' author. In my reading of Behn and her work, I argue that what these texts reveal is the fragility of not just white supremacy but any racial formation based on colorism because duplicity is ever possible.

If there is a goal or an aim to *Race and Romance: Coloring the Past*, it is to cast light on the racecraft that went into the making of romance a conduit for white supremacist illogic about the inherent stability of *race*. With the translation and publication into English of the first *interracial* romance novel, Heliodorus's *Aethiopica* and its subsequent adaptations, the romance genre has often been deployed to further English racism in subtle and not-so-subtle ways. Yet, with a few recent exceptions, it is rare to read scholarship on the complex intersection of race and romance even if we might assume otherwise given the advent of cultural studies, gender studies, and critical race studies and their impact on literary analysis. Much of this oversight may be laid at the doorstep of the "popular fiction versus literary fiction" debates that have shaped critical reception of the romance genre for most of the twentieth and twenty-first centuries.

Fighting such "literary wars" obscures what is strikingly similar about the racial politics of early modern romance and the recent debates on racism and the twentieth and twenty-first century English-language romance publishing industry. Namely, from the late sixteenth century forward, romance as a literary genre and a cultural ideology is projected through a decidedly "white," heterosexual, patriarchal, and classist lens. And, until recently, this reflection also seemed "writ in stone" within the romance reading and publishing industry. What hasn't been attended to, except tangentially, is the tangled web of historiography, racism, and colorism that mark not just the emergence of *race* and racial capitalism with respect to the romance genre, but the service to which romance novels have been put in fostering notions of white supremacy even as early as the sixteenth century. It is this "service," or racecraft, that is the central focus of *Race and Romance: Coloring the Past*.

Chapter One

Debating the Obvious

In an odd twist of fate, for most of the twentieth and twenty-first centuries the romance genre is routinely subject to disdain or dismissal as *popular or genre fiction* rather than literary fiction. The tone of dismissal varies. Robert Gottlieb's sarcastic commentary is probably more biting than most:

> Regency, psychopaths, wedding planners, ranchers, sadists, grandmas, bordellos, dukes (of course); whips, fish tacos, entails, Down syndrome, recipes, orgasms — romance can absorb them all, which suggests it's a healthy genre, not trapped in inflexibility. Its readership is vast, its satisfactions apparently limitless, its profitability incontestable. And its effect? Harmless, I would imagine. (Gottlieb 2017)

Diane Callahan's efforts to explain the differences between genre fiction and literary fiction lack the vitriol of Gottlieb's, even if her observation seems to affirm the sentiments behind Gottlieb's dismissal of romance:

> Beyond purpose and plot scale, to me the most distinctive marker between the two categories is writing style. *Genre fiction often uses more accessible prose* that reaches a wider audience and doesn't distract from the story being told. *Literary fiction values carefully crafted sentences* that can take more work to understand, but they attempt to capture precise images and feelings; they are often lyrical and layered. (Callahan 2020, original emphases)

In a *New York Times Books Review* interview, author Philippa Gregory denounces what she refers to as "lazy, sloppy genre novels" (Tamaki, 2017). Gregory ends her criticism by stating, "choosing to write a genre novel is like fencing the universe because you are afraid of space." Allison Flood, in a *The Guardian* response to Gregory's criticism, writes, "quite apart from the fact that every piece of writing falls into one genre or another, the comment is bizarre first because of who Gregory is. The author of *The Other Boleyn Girl*, *The Taming of the Queen*, and most recently *The Last Tudor*, Gregory writes historical fiction — and is indisputably a genre novelist herself" (Flood 2017). In fact, as Flood observes, "[i]t becomes even more bizarre when, in the same interview, Gregory goes on to name her favourite fictional hero as a Georgette Heyer gent: Vidal, in *Devil's Cub*." Flood concludes her commentary by wryly noting, "So Gregory clearly enjoys reading 'lazy, sloppy' genre writing herself. It's also a miscalculation because I'd say the readers of her books include a vast swath of romance readers. Romantic relationships between the kings and queens of yore are generally at the heart of Gregory's novels."

Within the genre itself, "self-proclaimed" romance authors seem to have trouble avoiding the "genre fiction" pitfalls. Elizabeth Reid Boyd titles the essay she wrote for *The Guardian* on February 13, 2017, "Trashy, Sexist, Downright Dangerous? In Defence of Romantic Fiction" with a preamble of "Dr Elizabeth Reid Boyd spent publication day of her first romance novel in a darkened room. She has since discovered there's nothing to be ashamed of" (Boyd 2017). Even the romance genre's fiercest advocates appear to reinforce this logic with titles such as *A Natural History of the Romance Novel*, *Historical Romance Fiction*, *New Approaches to Popular Romance Fiction*, *Making Meaning Popular Romance Fiction*, and *Happily Ever After: The Romance Story in Popular Culture*. Why not "romance genre" or "romance literature"? Why terms such as "fiction" or "story"? Of these titles, *A Natural History of the Romance Novel* is one that gestures toward the literary history of romance genre.

What is strikingly implicit in these academic book titles is an inescapable tie to academic ideologies about the cultural "purpose" of fictive writing. Often viewed as a guilty pleasure, for women only, and a misleading depiction of gender relations, romance has had more than its share of negative press over the course of its modern history. During the early modern period, the genre also received praise for its positive depictions of male and female virtue even as it was condemned for its frivolity. Caught between the rock, literature, and a hard place, genre fiction of the worst sort, the romance genre has had a contentious existence. Part of the issue lies in romance's generic fluidity: is it a genre, a literary mode, or merely a literary convention similar to metaphor or trope? Is romance an emotional state of being tied to relationships that are sexual in nature but inevitably lead to the protagonists "falling in love and enjoying a happily ever after" life? Or, is romance all of these and therein lies the problem?

Several factors contribute to the ways in which literary critics and academic scholars approach the romance novel. First, there is the implicit notion of literary canonicity and what texts are rightly labeled "literature" or "artistic" and what texts are relegated to the arena of popular fiction or "entertainment." The trivializing or belittling of the romance genre is not a recent phenomenon that occurs every February or when a "literary critic" or an author decides to mark territory. When we trace the historical debates about the complex relationships between epic, romance, and history, we find that writers themselves were not only ambivalent but also concerned as to the social or cultural value of romances. George Puttenham dismisses the romance as a "historical ditty," (Puttenham 1968/1589, 33) declaring that "[r]omances or historical rimes [are] made purposely for [the] recreation of the common people at Christmas dinners and bridals, and in taverns & alehouses and such other places of base resort" (83).

Torquato Tasso's *Discorsi dell'arte poetica* offered a challenge to those who claimed that romance and epic are distinct poetic forms, arguing "that since [he finds] no essential difference between the epic and the romance, it clearly follows that there is no generic distinction between them" (Rhu 1993, 121). For Tasso, "the romance (the name they use for *Orlando Furioso* and the like) is a kind of poetry different from epic, unknown to Aristotle, and therefore not bound by Aristotle's rules for epic" (Tasso 1973/1594, 68). Drawing upon Horace, Tasso contends that "those poems are better that win more approval from custom ... And custom prefers the kind of poetry called romance, which therefore must be judged the better" (68). Clearly, Philip Sidney and Edmund Spenser in writing *The Arcadia* and *The Faerie Queene* respectively indicate a preference for Tasso and Ariosto over the dictates of theorists such as Puttenham.

Other Renaissance and early modern English writers also found the romance genre in prose form (especially in the romance novellas of Bandello [c. 1480–1562] and Cinthio [1504–1573]) to be a much more fruitful and lucrative source for their interventions in the production of literature. In its various modes, the romance provided plots and characters that English writers often deployed in their drama and prose fiction. Works such as John Lyly's *Euphes* or George Gascoigne's *The Adventures of Master F.J.* helped to legitimate prose fiction as an acceptable heir apparent to the romance in poetic mode, and thus give rise to the modern novel. At least one twentieth-century scholar, A. C. Hamilton laments this evolution: "Elizabethan prose fiction was succeeded by the novel. That devourer and confounder of all literary genres corrupts the taste for romance by setting up demands for realism, correspondence to every-day experience, and a serious criticism of life which the former [romance] cannot satisfy" (Hamilton 1984, 23). Even so, Hamilton continues, "of course, romance was never superseded" by the novel, it "only went underground" (24). What Hamilton alludes to in his condemnation of the novel is a long-standing tension about the romance genre, its nature, and its ideological or cultural purposes.

Throughout the sixteenth century, and even into the seventeenth century, the complicated and conflicting relationship between the romance genre and historiography — tension alluded to in Puttenham's description — remained relatively intact. That is, despite describing their texts as "trifles" or "toys," early modern writers of the romance often envisioned their texts as engaging in the practice of historiography, albeit a bit more imaginatively drawn than the type of factual histories produced by chronicle writers. Romance authors engaging the crux of history as epic and the nature of romance were no longer emphatically insisting that their romances fell squarely into place as History. Equally, with the growing popular interest in the novella, the verse epic mode of narratively creating storylines began losing ground as the privileged site for the romance genre. An emerging non-aristocratic readership, publication costs, and the constraints of verse form opportunity may have contributed to a rapidly shifting preference for the prose form of romance.

This cultural shift, however, did not deter writers and theorists from attempting to both define and construct the romance text as a continuation of epic historiography. For example, in his preface to *Parthenissa: A Romance in Four Parts* (1655), Roger Boyle writes,

> All the Readers of Parthenissa may wonder at my making of Spartacus and Perolla contempories, & that Artabbanes & Spartacus

should be the same Person &c. But I hope [they] will no longer do so, when I Mind [remind] them, that I write a Romance, not a History, and that therefore though *all* I Relate be not the Truth, yet if a Part be, I perform more than what the title of my Book does confine me to. (Boyle 1953/1655, a3–4)

Though not entirely abandoning its claim to historical narrativity, romance was deemed to be, as Pierre Daniel Huet would write in 1670, "Fictions of Low Adventures, disposed into an Elegant Style in Prose, for the Delight and Instruction of the Reader" (Huet 1970/1715, 46). Unlike Huet, Georges de Scudery seeks to retain romance's claim to historical narrativity (de Scudery 1952/1674). After a brief discussion of the structural rules associated with romance in his preface to *Ibrahim, or the Illustrious Bassa*, de Scudery highlights what he considers to be the most significant: "but amongst all the rules which are to be observed in the compositions of these works, that of true resemblance is without question the most necessary; it is, as it were, the fundamental stone of this building" (3). He then notes that, in his own work, he has "observed the Manners, Customs, Religions, and Inclinations of People: and to give a more true resemblance to things, I have made the foundations of my work Historical, my principal Personages such as are marked out in the true History for illustrious persons, and the wars effective" (4).

 de Scudery's theoretical concept of the romance genre does not entirely settle the debates on its function, however. How is the reader supposed to comprehend a text that is described as a romance yet is also called a history? And what is the "verisimilitude" or "true resemblance" that writers presume or believe that they are invoking as history in their romances, and that the readers ought immediately or intuitively to comprehend? On the one hand, these questions are not entirely answerable as it is the very nature of romance to generate "error" and digression as the structural, even functional, principle of the romance mode (Parker 1979). Hence, most scholarly theories and analyses of romance accept that there is an inherent difficulty in attempting to define romance and instead address its "functional literary life," which involves a series of "generic transformations over time resulting in a kind of dynamic continuum" (Brownlee and Brownlee 1985, 1). In his groundbreaking *Anatomy of Criticism*, Northrop Frye writes that

> the romance is nearest of all literary forms to the wish-fulfilment dream, and for that reason it has socially a curiously paradoxical role. In every age the ruling social or intellectual class tends to project its ideals in some form of romance, where the virtuous heroes and beautiful heroines represent the ideals and the villains the threats to their ascendancy (Frye 1957, 186).

To return to the question of definition, Patricia A. Parker cogently observes that

> one of the problems in discussing the form of romance has always been the need to limit the way in which the term is applied. I have chosen to approach the subject in a way which does not cover all the forms we call "romance" but may provide what a romance poet might call a "prospect" on them... Romance... therefore, is characterized primarily as a form which simultaneously quests for and postpones a particular end, objective, or object. (Parker 1979, 4)

Similarly, Corrine Saunders finds that "the genre of romance is impossible adequately to define," which "is not so surprising when we recall that the term finds its origins in the French word romanz, meaning simply literature written in the vernacular, the romance language of French" (Saunders 2004, 2). Nonetheless, Saunders astutely postulates, "perhaps it is not fanciful to view romance as a genre waiting to happen, a story already told, situated in those moments of classical writing, inherent in the earliest of fictions and fundamental to human nature" (2).

Romance structurally confounds as much as it organizes. In other words, romance is viewed as an adventure or quest located more often than not in "nature" and predicated upon the notion of a wandering heroic figure. Concepts such as salvation or redemption, realism, possibility, and punishment are thematic hallmarks of the romance plot, while love and a happily ever after are its generic conventions. In the end, what is important in these studies of the romance genre is the idea of the social act. Or, as Fredric Jameson argues,

> as for romance, it would seem that its ultimate condition of figura-
> tion, on which the other preconditions we have already mentioned
> are dependent — the category of worldness, the ideologeme of
> good and evil felt as magical forces, a salvational historicity — is to
> be found in a transitional moment in which two distinct modes of
> production, or moments of socioeconomic development, coexist.
> (Jameson 1981, 148)

In essence, romance appears to be "bound up with a complex, evolving, historical situation" and, consequently, "different romances in different historico-literary contexts call ... for methodological heterogeneity" (Jameson 1981, 148).

The reader of this chapter might well ask, in a book dealing with racism and colorism, why begin with a genealogy of scholarly theories on the romance genre? Does it really matter what form it takes if the conclusion is "different historico-literary contexts" create definitional ambiguity? Furthermore, if the genre's texts are "bound up with a complex, evolving, historical situation," then why view twentieth- and twenty-first romance fiction as outside the framework of Literature and cast the same cloak on pre-twentieth-century romance texts such as *Faerie Queen, Urania, Pride and Prejudice, The Blithedale Romance,* or the *Unfortunate Traveler*? Where in the canonical envisioning of Literature has literary scholarship failed with the romance genre?

I pose these questions not to answer them but to suggest that the romance genre has a longstanding and very complicated relationship to literary formation and its role since its inception in early modern English culture. One aspect of this relationship is how much the romance genre is bound up with racial capitalism, something most of the theorists ignore. When we look at early modern English romances, regardless of form, there is a pervasive engagement with race-making, whether it is tied to nation, ethnicity, or colorism — and sometimes all three. When we examine contemporary, i.e., twentieth and twenty-first century romances, there is no surprise in discovering that not much has changed.

"The Grecians, Who Have Been Our First Masters"

In his treatise on romance, de Scudery argues that any writer of romance should look to "the Grecians, who have been our first Masters" (de Scudery 1952/1674, 2). One of the most influential of these "Greek masters" was Heliodorus, whose romance novel *Aethiopica* was translated and circulated in early modern English literary culture. Written between 230 and 275 CE, *Aethiopica* depicts the trials and tribulations of Charikliea, the daughter and heir of the monarchs of Ethiopia, and her beloved Theagenes, whose lineage is traceable to Achilles. Heliodorus is most likely indebted to the biblical account of the Ethiopian monarch Candace, which is taken up by Greek historiographers such as Pliny the Elder who writes

> They said that it [town of Meroe] is ruled by a woman, Candace, a name that has passed on through a succession of queens for many years .... At the present day there are reported to be forty-five other kings of Ethiopia. But the whole race was called Aetheria, and then Atlantia, and finally it took its name for Aethiops the son of Vulcan [universe vero gens Aetheria appellate est, deinde Atlantia, mox a Vulcani filio Aethiope]. (Pliny 1938/77 CE, 476–77)

The more famous Ethiopian princess who figures in *Aethiopica* and several adaptations of the romance novel is, of course, Andromeda.

For early modern romance theorists, Heliodorus's *Aethiopica* exemplifies all the conventions Renaissance and early modern English readers would come to love in their romance texts — pirates and armed men, caves and ambushes, dreams and visions, burnings, poisonings, and sudden deaths, battles and the triumph of virtue, and of course, love. The romance's depiction of virtues, such as chastity, honor, true love, and heroical figures, were consistently valorized as moral and ethical exempla in Renaissance and early modern English culture. As one Renaissance translator/editor observed: "not only many changes of fortune but also many images of virtue are here displayed. Among these is the description of Hydaspes, the king of Ethiopia, who is to be praised not only for his fortitude but also for his justice, clemency, and kindness towards those whom he has subdued" (quoted in Doody 1996, 237). In fact, "both in morality and taste, this book [was considered] irreproachable" by translators of Heliodorus's text (235). Not only was the *Aethiopica* translated from Greek into Latin, but it also appeared in Italian, French, German, and English versions. In England, the novel enjoyed extraordinary popularity and clearly left its mark on a reading populace hungry for both romances and novellas that went on well into the eighteenth and nineteenth centuries.

The assimilation of Heliodorus's text into English literary and cultural discourses was remarkable. The romance surfaced in translations, adaptations, and/or the appropriation of the romance's protagonists, Charikliea and Theagenes. *Aethiopica* appears to have achieved its popularity with writers and readers for a number of reasons. First, the text's humanist translators apparently held a high regard for Heliodorus's "sophisticated way of exploiting the varied interpretive practices of readers of narrative fiction" (Mentz 2006, 48). The novel also provided "an alternative to chivalric romance and the Italian novella" (48). In effect, Steve Mentz asserts, the "opening scene models the diverse relations between the text and the diverse practices of its readers" (48). At this point this assertion needs to be understood as speculation but the popularity of *Aethiopica* suggests readers seemed to have found great delight in Heliodorus's skillful handling of love, magic, and the fantastic, elements which enable the narrative to move metaphorically from the realm of the impossible and fantasy (romance) to the realm of the believable (realism or history).

Heliodorus's romance sets into motion a generic and historical context that came to shape not only the way romance was conceptualized but also what constitutes legitimate plotlines within the romance genre. However, because the *Aethiopica* makes use "of the Manners, Customs, Religions, and Inclinations of People ... to give a more true resemblance to things," (de Scudery 1952/1674, 4), the text's storyline proves to be a double-edged sword — it is simultaneously engaging and believable and ideologically disruptive of Renaissance and early modern English race-making. With the first English translation, Thomas Underdowne's, readers and authors become immersed in a shifting discourse about colorism and its growing ties to modern racism.

The inclusion of the white-presenting Ethiopian as the raison d'être for a romance was an original touch in Heliodorus's narrative. As a genre or mode that conventionalizes the fantastic or the supernatural, as well as the idea of happily ever after, romance was a fertile template for grasping the instability of race-making based on skin color. What theorists fail to consider is the way *Aethiopica* functions as an ideological conundrum that Renaissance and early modern European racism cannot entirely resolve. This is not to say that Heliodorus himself was free of what may best be described as racial prejudice; one has to only look at his representation of the Egyptians to discern his biases. Even so, the novel's aim seems not be the construction of an image of racial or ethnic negativity. Rather, the general purpose of the *Aethiopica* appears to be one of storytelling and the creative process of framing a readership. What the reader eventually discovers is that, had Charicles not insisted on arranging a marriage between Charikliea and his nephew, Charikliea's "Ethiopian" identity would most likely have remained a well-kept secret. Even when her true identity is revealed, no one evinces distaste or horror at Charikliea's Ethiopian-ness; for, as the novel makes clear, the Ethiopian people were held in high regard by the Greeks among whom Charikliea has lived.

At the novel's conclusion, Charikliea and Theagenes are wed and duly proclaimed heirs to the Ethiopian throne. Neither Charikliea's whiteness nor her parents' Blackness register as liabilities to Theagenes or, it appears, to Heliodorus and his readers. However, within the racializing taxonomy shaping sixteenth- and seventeenth-century England's view of the globe, such issues would prove problematic. Finally, and most importantly, what may have deeply intrigued and disconcerted English writers and readers of *Aethiopica* was the text's imaginatively constructed ideological dilemma and subsequent resolution with respect to Charikliea, a white-presenting Ethiopian.

Charikliea's Race

The appropriation and use of Heliodorus's *Aethiopica* as an illustrative text of idealized human behavior during the early modern period in England (and Europe) is not without irony. Despite the fact that Ethiopia had adopted Christianity as its principal religion in the early fourth century, "white" Europe did not truly take notice of the kingdom until the twelfth century. Moreover, while Ethiopia was a major economic player within the eastern Mediterranean region, it was the legend of Prester John that brought the African nation-state to Christian Europe's attention. The myth of Prester John, coinciding as it did with the religious wars between Islam and Christian Western Europe (typically referred to as the "Crusades"), led to further contact between European and Ethiopian Christians, and fostered the dream of a unified Christendom aligned against the followers of Islam (Saracens). By the beginning of the fifteenth century, relations (political and economic) were well-established between the courts of European monarchs and Ethiopia and, as a consequence of embassies and mercantile interactions, the geography, culture, commercial value, and political and religious practices of the African state became fairly well known to Renaissance and early modern Europe.

One of the most widely circulated texts across Europe to offer a picture of Ethiopia was A *Geographical Historie of Africa, Written in Arabicke and Italian by Iohn Leo a More, Borne in Granada, and Brought up in Barbarie* (published in 1600), which offered its readers a detailed account of Ethiopia. Leo, more commonly referred to as Leo Africanus, has this to say about Ethiopia:

> The Abassins have no great knowledge of Nilus by reason of the mountains which divide them from it; for which cause they call Abagni the father of rivers. Howbeit they say that upon Nilus do inhabit two great and populous nations; one of Jews towards the west, under the government of a mighty king; the other more southerly, consisting of amazons or war-like women; whereof we will speak more at large in our relation of Monomotapa. (Leo, 1969/1600, 13)

What stands out about Leo Africanus's discussion of Ethiopia is that it is atypical in the brevity of his description of the physical appearance of Ethiopians: "The people are scorched with the heate of the sun, and they are black, and go naked: save only that some cover their privities with cloth of cotton or of silk" (395). The rest of Leo Africanus's account about the Ethiopians focuses on their complicated status (to European eyes) as Christians. Ethiopian Christianity held to a different set of apostolic tenets including circumcision, adult baptism, holding the Sabbath on Saturday, and adherence to Coptic theology rather than that which governed the Vatican. In fact, European Christians apparently were quite disturbed by "their [the Ethiopians'] alien Judaizing religious practices ... [which] were unmistakably heretical" (Quint 1993, 236).

While the medieval Christian nation of Ethiopia remained an ideal to be exploited in the grand struggle against the "infidel" or pagan, the word that described the inhabitant of the Renaissance and early modern east African nation, Ethiopian, had lost its privileged Christian denotation. With increased contact between Europeans and Africans, especially sub-Saharan Africans, and the advent of the slave trade to provide labor for European settler colonies, the word Ethiopian joined Moor, Negro, and, African as part of a collapsible lexicon of racial demarcation. Furthermore, when Leo Africanus penned his *Geographical Historie of Africa*, this lexical conflation to mark Blackness virtually overrode all cultural and ethnic distinctions between and among African peoples, as well as differences between Eastern and Western Africa.

This lexical erasure, aided and abetted by a combination of ignorance and policy among European nations about the continent of Africa, isolated a single determinate — skin color — to racialize any person native to the continent. Ironically, despite its shared "Blackness" with "Negroes" and "Moors," Ethiopia remained very much a part of Christian culture. The effect, not surprisingly, was a cultural and historical paradox within European geopolitics that acknowledged Ethiopia's adherence to Christian doctrine even as it allowed for the people of Ethiopia to be racialized into Blackness (where Blackness signified alienness, inferiority, savagery or incivility, and evil) alongside other Africans. This paradigm was very much in play when, in 1569, Underdowne published the first English translation of Heliodorus's *Aethiopica* as *An Æthiopian Historie*. So popular was the translation that after a number of printing runs, Underdowne decided to produce an edition "newly corrected and augmented with divers and sundry new additions" in 1587 (Underdowne 1967/1587, 107).

In his preface to the "gentle reader," Underdowne writes that he reviewed the first translation and decided to "make it as perfect as" he "could, and to reform it from those so many horrible escapes" or errors that marred the first edition (4). He then goes on to "commend the reading of" his work, saying "If I shall compare it with other of like argument, I thinke none commeth near it. Mort Darthure, Arthur of little Britaine," and "Amadis of Gaule, etc, accompt violent murder, or murder for no cause, manhood: and fornication and all unlawfull lust, friendly love" (4). Heliodorus's text, Underdowne contends, "punisheth the faultes of evil doers, and rewardeth the well livers. What a king is Hidaspes? What a pattern of a good prince? What happy success had he? Contrariewise, what a lewd woman was Arsace? What a pattern of evil behaviour? What an evil end had she?" (4–5). Underdowne's commentary echoes sentiments articulated about Heliodorus's text.

Renaissance translations of *Aethiopica*, for the most part, adhered to the idea that a translation is merely the rendering of a foreign language text into the vernacular, and Underdowne's version was no different. When editors and translators of Heliodorus's romance intruded their views, it was generally in the form of an elucidation of a particularly difficult word or in marginal commentary on the ethical or moral lesson to be learned from a specific passage or chapter (as Underdowne's commentary makes clear). However, for English writers of fiction who later adapted portions of *Aethiopica*, or who "borrowed" from the work, the text's central premise may have presented them with something of a different quandary: do you leave intact the romance's representations of Ethiopia and Ethiopians, including the high regard with which they seem to be depicted by the Greek Heliodorus; or, do you "adapt" the image slightly so as not to completely denigrate Heliodorus's text yet making clear that the translator's culture holds a very different, and often ambivalent, view of Ethiopians? In other words, do you change Heliodorus's narrative to suit the generic aims of your own literary creativity and the cultural expectations of your society?

What goes unremarked in the cultural discourse surrounding *Aethopica*'s inclusion into early modern English fiction is the problems posed by the white-presenting Ethiopian. Unlike the white-passing subject, the white-presenting subject may or may not engage in the performative process of color passing for the simple reason of ignorance. Inherent in racial capitalism is a campaign of anti-Blackness that requires individuals to see Blackness, not whiteness as a racializing trope. To identify, or mark, a person's race, we are taught to look at biophysical externalities, skin, facial features, and, as if it is a genetic marker, geographical space. For Charikliea, none of her physical attributes (skin color and facial features) set her apart from the Greeks. Her father is Greek, his skin color is "white," and his socioeconomic status is enough to guarantee the perception and privilege of Charikliea's whiteness. Even when the "truth" of her birth and thus "race" become known, her white-presenting subjectivity is not a problem in Heliodorus's novel. However, the same cannot be said for adaptations and retellings of the romance of Charikliea and Theagenes.

In the next chapter, we will see what happens when early modern English racism meets Helidorus's romance and the racecraft doesn't entirely mesh. Focusing on two seventeenth-century English texts that retell significant elements of *Aethiopica*, Edward Fairfax's *Godfrey of Bulloigne* (a translation of Torquato Tasso's 1581 *Gerusalem Liberata*) and William Lisle's *The Fair Ethiopian* (1631), I discuss the ways Renaissance and early modern English writers came to terms with the "white-presenting Ethiopian." In different ways, each verse romance reveals its literary descent and its ideological distance from *Aethiopica*. My reading of Fairfax's and Lisle's poems argues that Heliodorus's female protagonist, Charikliea, cannot function as an ambiguous signifier of race as she does in Aethiopica. England's political economy, with its settler colonialist ideologies and its involvement in the enslavement of African peoples, cannot tolerate such ambiguity. English racism requires not just a hierarchy of colorism; it also requires that the hierarchy centers an anti-Blackness ideology. In other words, what the adaptations of *Aethiopica* do is rewrite the conventions of romance according to white supremacist logic.

Chapter Two

So Like Her Father

> Cario bragges and sweares his wife's a maide,
> Louely Lucrece, or Diana rather:
> Some sacred Saint in womans clothes arraide,
> And why? His children are so like their father:
> Yet Cario's cousoned, do what e're he can,
> She thinks of him, lies with another man.
>
> (Weever 1922/1599, 8)

In 1600, *Godfrey of Bulloigne, or the Recoverie of Jerusalem. Done into English Heroicall verse*, by Edward Fairfax, Gent., became the first English translation of the complete text of Torquato Tasso's 1581 epic romance, *Gerusalem Liberata*. According to its editors, *Godfrey of Bulloigne* is a "very free translation"; that is, Fairfax's text is not an exact rendering of Tasso's poem, rather it seeks to produce a "readerly" version of the poem (Fairfax 1981/1600). Of the extant adaptations of and borrowings from Heliodorus's *Aethiopica*, Tasso's *Gerusalem Liberata* reflects an author's decision to adapt the text to coincide with cultural ideologies and, in the narrative retelling of Heliodorus's love story, to change the ending. *Gerusalem Liberata* first appeared in 1580 in a pirated version, then in 1581 in an authorized publication. Within two decades, English writers were translating and/or borrowing from Tasso's text. In 1594, Richard Carew (translator) "offered readers the first part of 'An Heroicall Poem' by Torquato Tasso" (Fairfax 1981/1600, 20). Other writers influenced by Tasso's epic romance include Edmund Spenser, whose Book Twelve of the *Faerie Queene* is clearly indebted to Tasso's heroine, Clorinda.

Godfrey of Bulloigne takes as its subject matter one of the most long lasting conflicts in human history — the military, ideological, and political tension between Christianity and Islam. In the poem, Heliodorus's Charikliea is recast as the female warrior Clorinda and Theagenes surfaces as the Christian knight Tancred. Like Charikliea, Clorinda is fierce in her defense of her virtue, and once she falls in love with Tancred, she becomes a romantic emblem of fidelity and chastity. Where the two heroines differ is in their attitude towards warfare. On the one hand, Charikliea wears armor only to defend herself and her virtue. Clorinda, on the other hand, discovers a passion for battle and dedicates herself to it. Even so, she is not oblivious to her status as a maiden. Among her retinue, Clorinda travels with a Eunuch and several maids and though this detail affirms her as an ideal of chastity, the reader is not allowed to forget her attendants are Egyptians.

When the reader is first introduced to Clorinda in Book II, our heroine is described as "a warriour bold vnwares approched neare, / In vncouth arms yclad and strange disguise, / From countries far but new arrived there, / A savage tigress on her helmet lies" (Fairfax 1981/1600, 2:38). In the next line we discover that this image is "the famous badge" by which she was "well known," signaling both her ferocity and great cunning in battle. The next stanza reveals more about Clorinda's personality; she refuses all things "feminine" — "her lofty hand would of itself refuse / To touch the dainty needle, or nice thread" — and she engages in jousts, hunts, and the training of horses (2:39). The narrative stops short of reproducing Heliodorus's unwarlike heroine since Charikliea has patriarchal guardians while Clorinda answers to no patriarchal or masculine authority except her liege Soliman, the Egyptian ruler for whom she has taken up arms. Initially, the differences between the two romance heroines is enough to appear insignificant except for two telling moments. The first occurs when Fairfax recounts the lineage of one of the non-Christian women, Armida. The second moment is when Clorinda's lineage is revealed by Arsetes.

As the war rages on, Satan decides to intervene on behalf of the Egyptian army and sends his "neece" Armida on a mission of seduction. When she is brought before Godfrey, Armida informs him and retinue of her lineage:

> Prince Arbilan that reigned in his life
> On fair Damascus, was my noble sire,
> Born of mean race he was, yet got to wife
> The Queen Chariclia, such was the fire

Of her hot love, but soon the fatal knife
Had cut the thread that kept their joys entire,
For so mishap her cruel lot had cast,
My birth, her death; my first day, was her last. (4:43)

This naming is unexpected yet at this point the connection to *Aethiopica* hasn't been entirely clear. This is no longer the case. Any parallels to Heliodorus's heroine is quickly negated by the naming of Armida's mother and the language that describes her relationship with Prince Arbilan. Queen Chariclia's husband is described as being of a "mean race," and their relationship is defined solely in sexual terms: "the fire / Of her hot love."

The naming of the Queen constitutes a doubling of her foreignness: she is Ethiopian and Damascene by marriage. As if to underscore this sense of otherness, Fairfax translates Tasso's "in minor sorte nacque" as "a mean race." Fairfax's use of the word "race" rather than "birth" (which is what the word *nacque* would signify) is an interesting semantic and semiotic choice. On the one hand, it is obvious that Fairfax intends to convey the sense of the word that conveys social status, indicating Arbilan's lineage is of a lesser order than Queen Chariclia (he is a prince to her queen). On the other hand, it is also clear that *nacque* is affected by its syntactical relationship to Damascus and thus its meaning is inflected by the word's ideological identification with two different geographical locations, Damascus and Ethiopia.

Armida's parentage symbolically gestures towards the embodiment of a problematic religious and racial (i.e., color) subjectivity. Her father's status as Prince of Damascus reveals his Islamic affiliation, while her mother's name bespeaks an Ethiopian heritage as Heliodorus's heroine who eventually becomes Queen of Ethiopia. Reading the semantic intersections of non-Christian nomenclature within *Godfrey of Bulloigne*, we cannot but help noticing the ideological shift that takes place vis-à-vis Ethiopia in the poem. None of the Ethiopians in *Godfrey of Bulloigne* are depicted as Christians. In fact, the Ethiopians, led by Assimiro of Meroe (the southern and Islamic part of Ethiopia) fight on the side of Soliman and his warriors. It is this specificity that Armida draws attention to when she speaks her mother's name, not the Christian northern Ethiopia or the Hellenic understanding of Ethiopia that frames Heliodorus's novel. What the poem is doing is localizing Ethiopia in terms of Blackness and Islam.

David Quint asks of Tasso's epic romance, and the question has bearing on Fairfax's translation, "why is Clorinda an Ethiopian?" (Quint 1993, 235). The answer, Quint posits, lies in the complex interplay between the Renaissance engagement with the epic tradition and the religious politics that defined late medieval and Renaissance Europe. Despite its long historical engagement with Christianity, Ethiopia remained a divided state: the southern portion aligned with Islam while the northern part practiced a Coptic form of Christian theology. At the same time, the Ethiopian has a "literary genealogy" that marks their alien-ness vis-à-vis the "West" and, importantly, Christianity (Quint 1993). In most depictions, Renaissance literature engaged the Ethiopian as part of a somatic spectrum of "a sliding scale of skin color" where the Ethiopian represented the darker end of the scale (Brakke 2001). Yet the visual representations stood at odds with this normative representation as Elizabeth McGrath illustrates in her study of the artistic renderings of the Ethiopian female signifier that stands behind Heliodorus's romance, Andromeda. As McGrath writes,

> for his white Ethiopian Andromeda Heliodorus was probably influenced by images he had seen of the rescue by Perseus, such as those which survive in ancient paintings and mosaics. He was probably influenced too by the ekphrastic descriptions of pictures of the subject by Hellenistic writers; for even though these accounts universally locate the event in Ethiopia — and regard it as a part of Africa — they either imply or explicitly state that Andromeda is pale-skinned. (McGrath 1992, p. 2–3)

Renaissance and early modern artists, on the other hand, offered a range of Ethiopian Andromedas — from "European" to clearly sub-Saharan African in features and color (Galer Smith 2019).

The plates included in McGrath's essay reflect the variants in depiction. In Hendrick Goltizus's 1583 painting, Andromeda is clearly "white," while in Abraham van Diepenbeeck's 1632–35 painting, Andromeda's skin is darker and her hair distinctly curly or wavy. J. J. von Sandrart's "Rescue of Andromeda" offers the most explicitly "Black" Andromeda (McGrath 1992,

Plates 1–3, respectively). One of the more intriguing renditions is that of van Diepenbeeck, who produced his illustration sometime during his stay in Paris. The illustration was commissioned by Jacques Favereau for a book of illustrations probably based on Ovid's *Metamorphoses*. Michel de Marolles assumed responsibility for the project upon Favereau's death and the work was published with the title *Tableaux du Temple des Muses* in 1655. van Diepenbeeck's illustration was roundly condemned by Marolles

> for showing the heroine this way without, according to [Marolles], any ancient authority. [Marolles] admits that Andromeda "was perhaps from a *black family*, being an Ethiopian but expresses amazement that the artist has shown her with "a Moorish colour", for she was the most beautiful woman alive, so that presumably she would have been white, albeit African. After all, he notes, the learned Heliodorus made Chariclea both Ethiopian and white. In any case, he continues, the ancient poets would obviously have mentioned it, had Andromeda really been dark-skinned. (McGrath 1992, 13, emphasis added)

Quint's argument that Tasso's "Clorinda is clearly a composite of ... two figures" drawn from Virgil's *Aeneid*: "the Ethiopian Memnon, the son of the goddess Dawn, and Penthesilea, queen of the Amazons," both of whom were killed by Achilles, only makes sense if we ignore the complications of the visual and narrative framework generated by Clorinda's links to Andromeda (Quint 1993, 238–39). Where Quint's analysis succeeds is in suggestively reading Clorinda as part of the papal intervention in Ethiopian Christianity. If, as Quint asserts, the Ethiopian is the heretical interiority of Christianity, then Clorinda as a "white" European "soul in search of baptism" does not produce the same exegetical impact as a "white" Ethiopian "soul in search of baptism" (243). What seems so significant about the Ethiopian that it had to be incorporated into Tasso's plot, and into the main love relationship in the text, is that the figure, Black and Christian, represents the paradoxical subject that cannot be assimilated nor ignored. In effect, the answer to Quint's question is accounted for in *Godfrey of Bulloigne* when the reader *and* Clorinda discover the truth of Clorinda's lineage, and the clear destabilization that a living Clorinda threatens. Clorinda's subjectivity becomes the interdiction of Heliodorus's "passing" narrative and the generic and ideological possibilities it holds for Renaissance Christian societies. Clorinda is a white-presenting Ethiopian, to return to Quint's query, because of racism and an ideology of colorism that makes her white supremacy's greatest fear, the unrecognizable Black subject.

The White-presenting Ethiopian

Kept awake by her "working thought, / Which thirsted still for fame and warlike praise" (Fairfax 1981/1600, 12:2), but aware of the limits her gender imposes, Clorinda decides to put to rest her "thoughts ... full of ... strange desire" (2:5). To Argantes, who has "accompanied the maid, / From place to place," she reveals her plan to secretly enter the Christian war camp and set fire to the towers. Acutely conscious of the dangers she faces in undertaking the mission, Clorinda gives her household into the care of her constant companion, the warrior Argantes: "But if it fortune such my chance should be / That to this town I never turn again, / Mine Eunuch (whom I dearly love) with thee / I leave, my faithful maids, and all my train" (12:6). Argantes refuses, declaring that her "fellow have I been in arms, / And will be still, in praise, in death, in harms" (12:7).

After consultation with Soliman, the king, who approves the plan, Clorinda returns to her chamber and

> there her silver arms off rent
> Her helm, her shield, her hauberk shining bright,
> An armour black as jet or coal she hent,
> Wherein without plume her self she dight;
> For thus disguis'd amid her foes she meant
> To pass unseen by help of friendly night. (12:18)

Arsetes ("her Eunuch old"), discovering her intent, endeavors to dissuade her from the mission. When it is clear that his pleas have failed, Arsetes tells Clorinda to "Attend a while, strange things unfold I will; / Hear both thy birth and high estate declar'd" (12:20).

It is here that the clearest appropriation of Heliodorus's narrative about Charikliea's racial identity surfaces. In this storytelling, the only changes made are to the principal characters' names, religious beliefs, and the description of the painting that hangs in the Ethiopian Queen's chamber. Arsetes informs Clorinda that her parents are royalty and her father, Senapus, "rul'd, and yet perchance doth reign / In mighty Ethiopia and her deserts waste." In addition, Arsetes informs her that "the lore of Christ both he [Senapus] and all his train / Of people black, hath kept and long embraced" (12:21). Arsetes then relates the circumstances of Clorinda's birth and how she came to perceive herself as an Egyptian:

> 12:23
> Her prison was a chamber, painted round
> With goodly portraits and with stories old,
> As white as snow there stood a virgin bound,
> Besides a dragon fierce, a champion bold
> the monster did with poinant speare through wound,
> The gored beast lay dead upon the mold;
> The gentle queen before this image laid,
> She plain'd, she mourn'd, she wept, she sigh'd she prayed:

> 12:24
> At last with child she proved, and forth she brought
> (And thou art she) a daughter fair and bright,
> In her thy colour white new terror wrought,
> She wondered on thy face with strange affright;
> But yet she purposed in her fearful thought
> To hide thee from the king thy father's sight,
> Least thy bright hue should his suspect approve,
> For seldom a crow begets a silver dove.

> 12:25
> And to her spouse to show she was disposed
> A negro's babe, late born, in room of thee,
> And for the tower wherein she lay enclosed
> Was with her damsels only one and mee,

To me, on whose true faith she most reposed,
She gave thee, ere thou couldest christened bee.

Clearly a storyteller, Arsetes provides both Clorinda and the epic's readers greater insight into Clorinda's childhood and what motivates her warlike actions. Arsetes's narrative extends for another fifteen stanzas and includes a number of fantastic details (a tigress who nursed Clorinda, friendly winds, and dreams) about his endeavors to fulfill his promise to Clorinda's mother to keep the royal princess safe and to see her baptized as a Christian — only the latter promise has not been fulfilled.

A look at Thomas Underdowne's translation of the same plotline in *Aethiopica* reveals the level of transformation Heliodorus's denouement undergoes in *Godfrey of Bulloigne*, however. In Underdowne's text, Calasiris, the Egyptian eunuch to whom Charikliea's mother entrusted her daughter, is called to Charikliea's adoptive father's (Caricles) home. Caricles has attempted to wed his daughter to his "sisters sonne"; however, Charikliea, in love with Theagenes, refuses and threatens suicide if her adoptive father attempts force. Calasiris, recognizing that "some God taketh on him to hinder this businesse," asks Caricles to show him Charikliea's "fascia" or a band of cloth worn to indicate status. Upon the fascia "were Æethiopian letters, not common, but suche as the princes use, which are like the letters that the Egyptians use in their holy affayers" (Underdowne 1967/1587, 107). The writing proves to be a letter from "Persina, Queene of the Aethiopians to her daughter" (107). The letter tells of Persina's infertility, her pregnancy, and the circumstances of her daughter's birth:

> After Hidaspes had bene married to me ten years, and we had never a child, we happened to rest after dinner in the summer, for that we were heavy a sleep, at which time your father had to do with me, swearing that by a dream he was commanded to do so, and I by and by perceived my self with child.... But thou were born white, which color is strange amonge the Aethiopians: I knew the reason, because I looked upon the picture of Andromeda naked, while my husband had to do with me. (107–108)

The frightened Queen tells Hidaspes that the child was born dead, then "privily laid thee forth, with the greatest riches that [she] had, for a reward to him that shall find thee, and take thee up" (108).

Persina's anxiety and fear, not surprisingly, reflects her internalization of longstanding patriarchal anxieties about women's sexuality. The Queen rightly intuits the outcome that Charikliea's incredulous birth will engender should she present the child to the king; thus her only recourse to protect both her honor and the life of her child is the deception she undertakes. Persina's solution, however, is a temporary one as Heliodorus's romance makes clear. The abandoned child, now an adult and with full knowledge of her lineage and racial history, returns to claim her identity. Heliodorus produces the necessary romance denouement while at the same time underscoring the idea that all generative anomalies can be explained. The story of Persina became part of medical lore on reproduction. In *The Works of that Famous Chirugeon Ambrose Parey*, Ambroise Paré uses the story of Persina to illustrate the various types of anomalies that can arise in the process of reproduction (Paré 1678). Two sections of Paré's Oeuvres focused specifically on issues related to human generation, male and female sexuality, and the nature or properties of "seed" or semen.

In Books 24 and 25, Paré undertakes to clarify for his readers the philosophical debates about the process of generation and its properties. In particular, Paré is concerned that his readers have a precise understanding of what exactly is the nature of "seed." According to Paré, "in the seed lieth both the procreative and formative power. As for example, in the power of the melon-seed are situate the stalks, branches, leaves, flowers, fruit, form, colour, smell, taste, seed, and all" (535). Like numerous treatises before it, Paré's work finds the agricultural analogy most useful for framing his explanation of the importance of seed to generation. Paré replicates classical and medieval assumptions about the differences and hierarchy that exist between male seed and female seed. In particular, Paré reiterates the idea that the sexual difference extant as a property of seed has serious implications for the production of children. Paré observes that

Children are more like the Father than the Mother, because that in the time of copulation, the mind of the woman is more fixed on her husband than the mind of the husband on, or towards his wife: for in the time of copulation or conception, the forms or the likeness of those things that are conceived and kept in mind, are transported and impressed in the child or issue (535).

Paré discusses such issues as the effect of the female imagination on reproduction, the significance of erotic foreplay to conception, and the need for mothers to nurse their infants as part of the general discussion of the seed's relation to the process of generation. In this explanation, Persina's story becomes the groundwork for an insistence on regulating the female imagination in relation to conception. As further evidence, he recounts the tale of Hippocrates who "saved a princess accused of adultery, because she had given birth to a child as Black as a Moor, her husband and she both having white skin; which woman was absolved upon Hippocrates' persuasion that it was [caused by] the portrait of a Moor, similar to the child, which was customarily attached to her bed" (Paré 1982/1573, 38). Paré then goes on to advise that "it is necessary that women — at the hour of conception and when the child is not yet formed (which takes thirty to thirty-five days for males and forty or forty-two, as Hippocrates says, for females) — not be forced to look at or to imagine monstrous things" (39–40).

The pervasiveness of Paré's theories continue well into the seventeenth century, in particular the idea of paternal resemblance. The English physician Helkiah Crooke takes up the issue of *semblance* in *Microcosmogria: A Description of the Body of Man* (Crooke 1651). Crooke asks, "Whence it cometh that Children are like their Parents?" Crooke begins philosophically,

as among Philosophers there is a three-fold form of every Creature: the first Specificall; the second of the Sex; and the third of the Individuum or particular by which it is that and no other thing: So among Physitians there is a three-fold similitude: the first in specie, i.[e.,] in the kind, the second in the Sex, the third in the fashion or feature or individual figure. (Book V, 225).

The third similitude, according to Crooke, consists of the "figure, Form, and Accidents of the Individuum. This Galen in his second Book De Semine, will have to consist in the differences of the parts, and in the conformation of the Members. By this one is white, another black, one hawk-nosed, another flat or saddle-nosed" (Book V, 226).

In other words, the third similitude is at work when the child resembles neither parent but some other relative or "unknown friend." Because of this "similitude," Crooke suggests, we find that

> The Infant sometimes is altogether like the Mother, sometimes altogether like the Father, other sometimes like them both, that is, in some parts resembling the Mother, in others the Father. Oftentimes he resembleth neither the Father nor the Mother, but the Grandfather or the great Grandfather, sometimes he will be like an unknown friend, as for example, an Æthiopian or such like who never had hand in his generation. Of all these similitudes wee have many Examples in Authors of approved credit. (Book V, 226)

For this reason, in the John Weever epigram that opens this chapter, Cario can publicly celebrate his wife's virtue, swearing she is a "maide" and comparing her to "Lucrece, or Diana," even though his children are fathered by another man (Weever 1922/1599). Cario's declaration is based on his belief that "his children are so like their father" in their appearance that there can be no question as to his wife's fidelity. Yet, the satiric conclusion of the epigram makes clear that Cario has been thoroughly cuckolded; his wife has in fact "cousoned" him, for "she thinks of him" as she "lies with another man."

Two points need to be made about the ideological implications of Weever's tale. First, the narrative highlights Cario's lack of familiarity with reproductive theories about generation; in spite of his evocation of Lucrece and Diana (emblems of chastity), his insistence that because the children look like him his wife's fidelity is proven is indicative of his gullibility. Cario's wife, on the other hand, clearly knows the prevailing theories on female imagination and conception. Second, despite the examples drawn from "authority" (whether Hippocrates, Galen, Paré, or Crooke), the narrative of Cario and his wife identifies an underlying nervousness about paternity that is not easily suppressed. For a woman to commit adultery is problematic enough. For her to pass another man's offspring into her husband's line is alarming, especially if the child's physical appearance cannot be accounted for through paternal resemblance. Ironically, what distinguishes the experience of Cario's wife and Persina is not an active imagination but the matter of skin color.

Heliodorus's romance resolves the dilemma of resemblance and paternity by ensuring that despite her whiteness Charikliea is patrilineally recognizable through a literal physical signifier (a black mark on her arm). Acknowledged by her "Black" father, Charikliea and Theagenes are incorporated into the Ethiopian royal family as Hiadpses's heirs. As Judith Perkins writes, "the ending of the *Aethiopica* explicitly abolishes the antitheses of difference and concludes with a celebration of the unity of disparate elements" (Perkins 1999, 209). While the *Aethiopica* makes clear it is Charikliea's lineage not her color that matters in the end, it is her color and her race that condition Renaissance and early modern reactions to Heliodorus's romance. More to the point, it is the seeming invisibility of Charikliea's "Blackness" that needs to be perceptible and in conformity with the colorism surfacing in early modern conceptualizations of race. For the poet Tasso, who borrowed heavily from Heliodorus, and his English translator Fairfax, the solution was simple: change the ending.

Until Book 12, both Clorinda and the reader are ignorant of her racial and romance genealogies. Only when Arsetes narrates her "history" does the reader recognize the Heliodorian imprint. Unlike Charikliea, however, Clorinda refuses to embrace her Ethiopian identity — "I will this faith [Islam] obserue, it seemes me true, / Which from my cradle age thou taught me hast; / I will not change it for religion new" (Fairfax 1981/1600, 12:41). As long as Clorinda's Ethiopian or "Black" origin remains concealed, it is simultaneously a problem and not. Once Clorinda (and by extension, the reader) possess knowledge of her identity, her subjectivity is irrevocably altered. Repudiating her "Black" Ethiopian and Christian subjectivity, Clorinda chooses to remain as she is — a white-passing Egyptian. Even so, the knowledge of her newly discovered identity requires a visible sign, just as Charikliea's readmission into the Ethiopian royal family required a marker. Where Charikliea had a black birthmark to denote her relationship to Ethiopia's King and Queen, Clorinda has only Arsetes's tale.

Choosing black armor instead of her usual silver, Clorinda signals a discursive realignment in the narrative. The black armor functions on two levels: first, it literally conceals her identity as she enters and sets fire to the Christian camp; and second, it becomes the allegorical simulacrum for her "Blackness" — in other words, a second skin. A symbolic act of reversion, Clorinda's armor effaces the idealized image the poem has created and replaces it with an otherness that metaphorically ties her to Blackness and thus indistinguishable from the other women aligned with the Islamic forces. In the ideological mirror that the black surface of Clorinda's armor creates, we see Persina's failure to control her imagination; in the poet naming Armida's mother Chariclia, we witness the literary genealogy that ties Clorinda to Blackness and paganism; and finally, the necessity for Clorinda's subsequent albeit temporary appearance as a "demonic simulacrum" serves to remind Tancred of his religious and racial obligations.

Because *Godfrey of Bulloigne* frames Clorinda's whiteness within the religious and anti-Blackness ideologies that inform early modern English culture, the racecraft that worked in *Aethiopica* will not work for Clorinda. While Charikliea eventually becomes reunited with her parents and weds her beloved Theagenes, Clorinda never meets her Ethiopian parents. As to the romance's "happy ending," Clorinda is slain by her beloved Tancred — a love story that has been in state of perpetual deferral because of his Christianity and her allegiance to Islam. The couple's meetings for the most part take place on the battlefield and are both comical and poignant since the lovers fail to recognize each other until after they have exchanged blows. However, just when we, as readers, expect the lovers' dilemma to be resolved in typical romance fashion, the narrative thwarts our desire (just as it continually thwarts Tancred's) with the revelation of Clorinda's racial identity and decision to externalize what has been hidden most of her life.

> After a particularly fierce battle between Clorinda and Tancred,
> ... the fatal hour arrives,
> That her sweet life must leave that tender hold,
> His sword into her bosom deep he drives,
> And bathed in lukewarm blood his iron cold,

Between her breasts the cruel weapon rives
Her curious square, embossed with swelling gold. (Fairfax 1981/
1600, 12:64)

As she lies dying, Clorinda elects to convert to her parents' religion and asks Tancred to "save my soul, baptism I dying crave" (12:66). Tancred complies with her request, and she "smile[s] and sa[ys], 'I die in peace'" (12:68). Clorinda dies in the arms of the "white" Christian prince she loves, newly baptized into the Christian faith.

The death of Clorinda marks the end of one of the more powerful warriors in *Godfrey of Bulloigne* and signals the eventual success of the Christian knights against the Islamic forces defending Jerusalem. There is, in my view, one "end" that her death fails to achieve: the erasure of the problem that her Ethiopian origin intrudes upon the schematic of racial thinking in Renaissance and early modern European cultures — white passing. In part, this failure occurs because any literary translation, adaptation or evocation of Charikliea cannot help but elicit two sets of racializing codes associated with her place of birth and the skin color of her parents (not to mention Charikliea's white-presenting subjectivity). The first set of attributes are engrained in the cultural beliefs of the world Heliodorus inhabited, where a concept of racial identity was defined primarily along patrilineal and class lines. This isn't to say colorism wasn't an issue in Greek culture, just that Heliodorus apparently didn't view it as a deterrent to *Aethiopica*'s happily ever after. The second set of codes are those that tie race and colorism together and place them in the service of English white supremacy.

This factor makes it difficult to interpret Clorinda as anything other than a negative. As the epic battle between Tancred and Clorinda draws to an end, the language and imagery shifts. The mortally wounded heroine prays but, ironically, not to Islam but within a Christian frame: "A spirit new did her those prayers teach, / Spirit of hope, of charities, and faith; / and though her life to Christ rebellious were, / Yet died she his child and handmaid dear" (Fairfax 1981/1600, 12:65). Are we to read her death as the separation of body and soul so that her lineal and anti-Christian "Blackness" can be whitewashed, especially in light of the spectrum of African enslavement based on color and geography? I suspect the answer is no.

What is clear is that, for all her "whiteness," Clorinda cannot escape the stigma that her place of birth and her parents' skin color imposes on her subjectivity. The legitimacy of her suitability as a potential wife for Tancred, assuming her conversion to Christianity, is called into question not only by the details of her birth but also by the contradictions created by those details. Clorinda cannot be neatly categorized: she is "neither black nor white yet both"; she is both marked and unmarked, her body readable and unreadable.

It is this unreadability that Charikliea introduces into early modern English adaptations and translations of Heliodorus's romance. Perkins argues, as a "passing" narrative, Heliodorus's *Aethiopica* "functions ... to interrogate the whole notion of 'identity' as a given either/or dichotomy, a given ontological condition" (Perkins 1999, 198). Furthermore, for Perkins, Heliodorus uses "the figure of the white maiden who is 'really' black as a trope to figure the permeability of a category even more constitutive of his Hellenic culture than white/black, that is the categorical opposition of Hellenic/other" (202). Charikliea becomes the bodily site where issues of legitimacy and racial/national identity become negotiated; and the reading of the fascia is the act that instantiated her relationship to Ethiopia and by extension to Blackness, and of course engenders a need for resolution. In other words, Perkins writes, "An Ethiopian who is not black must, by definition, not be an Ethiopian; she is a counterfeit" (208). Of course, Charikliea is both and Heliodorus's narrative "goal" is to prove that "identity ... to be not necessarily an either/or category — either real or counterfeit — but a both/and category — both different and legitimate" (208).

Nowhere is this more amply illustrated than when Sisimithres demands that Charikliea "bare" her arm, for "there is nothing indecent in laying bare that which will confirm your parentage and descent" (Reardon 1989, 569). Charikliea does so, revealing "a mark, like a ring of ebony staining the ivory of her arm!" Of this denouement, Perkins cogently observes, "the dictum that it is never 'unseemly' ... to show the proof of your parentage and race ... may resonate for all those 'passing' in Greco-Roman culture" (Perkins 1999, 208). In his translation, Underdowne describes Charikliea's identifying mark as being "in a manner a mole, much like to the strakes [strips] that Elephants have" (Reardon 1989, 569).

The assimilation of Heliodorus's romance into seventeenth-century English literary texts created an interesting dilemma for Aethiopica's adapters and appropriators where the political and cultural economy of the transatlantic slave trade narrowed and constrained the racial significance of colorism. In the introduction to Critical White Studies, the editors begin with what seems a straightforward question: "Are you white? (Or, do you have a friend who is?) If so, how do you know?" (Delgado and Stefancic 1997, xvii). While early modern authors may not have explicitly posed these questions as the driving force behind their use of Heliodorus's romance, English writers who made use of Aethiopica implicitly endeavored to answer these questions for their audience. The shift to "scientific" reasoning and measurements for racial taxonomies — somatic and physiological markers — contributed greatly to the ideology of colorism that marks early modern preoccupation with whiteness. However, if whiteness is to be seen as the "privileged marker" of racial identity within early modern England's political economy and thus needs no explanation, how does one deal with the problematics created by Heliodorus's Aethiopica?

Not surprisingly, Heliodorus provides an answer through a suggestive reading of Charikliea's white-presenting body as the eloquent articulation of interiority and, I would argue, this is the reading Fairfax/Tasso must grapple with in their appropriation. To deal with the conundrum that is a white-presenting, Black body, writers made use of the one central tell in early modern English literature for marking whiteness — the ability to blush. In other words, to foreground the invisibility of whiteness it must be made visible. The reader is frequently reminded of Charikliea's color through blushes, paleness, and the familiar comparison to lilies. The blush, the paleness, and the flower tropes serve to heighten not just the Ethiopian Charikliea's proximity to "whiteness" but also her distance from Blackness. In a curious turn, the presumed invisibility of the "blush" on Black skin reinforces this intriguing sleight of hand within the ideology of colorism. Naturally, in a historical and economic moment, the seventeenth century, where Blackness functions as negative, Charikliea's ability to blush becomes an investment in the anti-Blackness at the center of English white supremacy. In the end, despite the historical context embedded in Godfrey of Bulloigne, the text remains caught in the nexus of *Aethiopica*'s romance ending through its appropriation of Heliodorus's heroine even as early modern England's political economy conceptualizes and interprets racial identity differently.

Unlike the Fairfax/Tasso poem, William Lisle's *The Faire Æthiopian* (1631) and its dramatic offspring, John Gough's "trage-comedie" *The Strange Discovery* (1640), were based on Underdowne's translation. Because Gough's "trage-comedie" adheres closely to Lisle's *The Faire Æthiopian*, I want to focus attention on Lisle's text and the several references to Chariclea's shifting skin color (i.e., the ability to blush or grow pale): "Chariclia's colour went and came the while" (Book X, 725); "Her colour's gone, her all-delighting grace / With pearly shower allayed" (Book III, 268–69); "your colour, here so peregrine, / Doth plainly show you can be none of mine. / Then said Sisimithres, the child was white" (Lisle 2011/1631, Book X, 725). Because Lisle's verse romance remains consistent with Heliodorus's text, Chariclia's race becomes visible only when she is reunited with her Ethiopian parents and successfully proves her chastity by enduring a trial by fire and, after doing so, declares Hydapses to be her father:

> But of Blood royal, to your self full near.
> The King it scorned, and her, for words so vain
> And new devised; she reports again,
> With sober countenance and behavior mild;
> Most royal father scorn not so your child! (Book X, 294–98)

The angry king admits that he had a daughter but she "quickly" died. Chariclia then tells Hydapses that she will present "two kinds of Arguments, as I am told, / are chiefly used in proof: the first enrolled by writing are, the second firmly stand on witness unexcepted on either hand" (Book X, 311–14).

Chariclia offers her father the cradle band and letter her mother had placed with her. Sisimithres affirms Chariclia's account, telling the king, "I am he that took her from the Queene," and cared for the child for seven years before placing her with Charicles. Sisimithres explains that he took action to ensure that Hydapses leave an heir. Sisimithres then calls for the picture of Andromeda, Hydapses's ancestor, to be placed next to Chariclia and "all that looked on them admitting said; / O father know your child, mistrust not mother, / For, but by life, we know not the one from the other" (Book X, 400–402). Determined to leave no doubt in the king's mind, Sisimithres offers the final evidence to support Chariclia's claim:

> Royal Descent,
> And Crown, and Scepter is weighty consequent:
> And truth most weighty of all: another sign
> I know, may best the Imperial cause define.
> Your left arme (Lady) show; 'tis no disgrace
> To show a naked arme in such a case.
> If you be that same royal child I knew,
> Above your elbow a mark there is of blue.
> She showed, and so it was; like an [azure] ring
> On polished Ivory; this when saw the King,
> He was persuaded. (Book X, 407–17)

Convinced by the indisputable physical evidence (Chariclia's birthmark and her striking resemblance to Andromeda), the verbal affirmation of a trusted member of the Ethiopian court (Sismisthres), Charicles' account of his adoption and raising of Chariclia, and the Queen's claim of ownership of the letters and jewels that Chariclia presented as evidence, Hydapses acknowledges Chariclia as his daughter and heir.

The Faire Æthiopian's sense of itself as a verse translation of Heliodorus's ends with this familial reconciliation, yet Lisle seems concerned about letting the tale stand on its own merits. The lingering effects of Chariclia's white-presenting Blackness may have led Lisle to add a codicil to his verse poem in which he color codes the induction of Chariclia and Theagenes into the Ethiopian royal power structure:

> Then on their head he set in full renown,
> The white silk Turban with the Blakemore Crown:
> And two by two to Meroë they ride;
> Persina with her new-come daughter Bride;
> Hydaspes with his son Theagenes;
> And Priest of Delphos with Sisimithres:

> There are many days together and many nights
> They celebrate with joy the nuptial rites. (Book X, 891–98)

Newly incorporated into the Black "body politic" of Ethiopia, yet still somatically "white," Chariclia leaves open-ended the question of racial subjectivity. Is she "translated" by her incorporation into the Ethiopian community? Or does she symbolically circumvent the type of closure colorism was initiating within early modern racism? In the end, Lisle descriptively frames Chariclia's return to the Ethiopian community with language to signal her "Blackness": "the white silk Turban with the Blakemore Crown"; "A curly-head black-boy"; "Memnon, fair Aurora's son" — the Ethiopian warrior who fought on the side of the Greeks during the Trojan War; and Andromeda and Perseus, whose image set into motion Chariclia's history.

Ultimately, it is the Andromeda and Perseus narrative that stablizes the romance's miraculous storyline, creating a portrait of what "Ethiopian" can signify in a world where Black and white were becoming stable markers of racial subjectivity. In Lisle's romance, Andromeda's own Ethiopianness was being redefined so that Lisle's description of her "picture fair, in black King's chamber seen, / That Fair-one made be borne of Blackmore Queen" (Lisle, 913–914) stood in contrast to a shifting depiction of Andromeda in the visual arts, which may have given rise to is the presence of a Black Andromeda as part of Renaissance and early modern English literary culture. We have to wonder how influential *Godfrey of Bulloigne*, *The Faire Æthiopian*, and of course Underdowne's translation of *Aethiopika* may have influenced Nahum Tate to give late seventeenth-century English readers another translation of Heliodorus's romance: *The Triumphs of Love and Constancy a Romance, Containing the Heroick Amours of Theagenes & Chariclea: In Ten Books*, 1686).

That *Aethiopica* appeared in such a variety of generic forms attests to the early modern English reading public's obvious fascination with and consumption of Heliodorus's romance. What is also striking is that a text framed by an ideology of colorism and that illuminated the possibility of white passing, achieved such popularity in a world increasingly pushing an ideology of white supremacy as part of its global colonizing agenda. Perhaps these translators and adapters recognized, as Geraldine Heng has cogently argued, "romance ... as a genre of the nation: a literary medium that solicits or invents the cultural means by which the ... nation might be most productively conceptualized, and projected, for a diverse society of people otherwise ranged along numerous internal divides" (Heng 2003, 6). Although, it is ironic that while Heliodorus's *Aethiopica* offered the early modern English literary and cultural imagination both a remarkable genre, the romance, to "conceptualize" and "project" a national identity centered in "whiteness," it was Fairfax's *Godfrey of Bulloigne* that gave the cultural imagination license to police the white-passing body, and when all else failed, to kill off the Black body.

Chapter Three

Settling an Isle, or an Englishman's Color

Exilio 1599

Francisco Drake stood stoically as the rough noose slipped
over his head. As the rope tightened about his neck he
meditated on this, the day of his death — the end of his
exile. He felt no remorse for his actions, only a profound
regret that he would leave his wife and niño with no one to
care for them. His brown eyes looked over the crowd gath-
ered to watch him hang, finally discovering the tearful blue
ones of his wife. Her white face pale, she held his infant
daughter Elizabeth to her breast. His lips moved silently,
speaking only to her, a smile forming to soften his handsome brown face as she nodded her understanding. Francisco bent his head, refusing to speak to the crowd, and
the hangman earned his fee. *No mas desterrado.*
(Hendricks n.d., unpublished work)

Race is a phenomenon always in formation. Therefore
whiteness, like other racial constructions, is subject to
contest and change. Whiteness is historically located, mal-
leable, and contingent .... [and], like culture, race is something whites notice in themselves only in relation to
others.
(Mahoney 1997, 330–31)

In the aftermath of the English Civil War, the concept of race was to
acquire a logic that had escaped earlier ideologues of English racism.
Arguably, early modern ethnographers contributed much to England's
understanding of human difference; however, it would take the practi-
tioners of "the New Science" to fully instantiate a scientific framework for

the adumbration of racial differences. One of these new scientists was Robert Boyle. In his treatise, "The Experimental History of Colours, Part II. Of the Nature of Whiteness and Blackness," Boyle's expressed purpose is to account for the properties of color in a rational, scientific way (Boyle 1965/1772). The sections of Boyle's essay on color are organized according to two categories, "observation" and "experiment." For Boyle, the distinction between the two terms is crucial. Observation is not limited to the specular; it can also comprise the written and the oral explications of others. The experiment, on the other hand, occurs under carefully controlled circumstances, with technology, and verified by what we can call the "modest witness." Donna J. Haraway argues the "modest witness is the legitimate and authorized ventriloquist for the object world, adding nothing from his mere opinions, from his biasing embodiment. And so he is endowed with the remarkable power to establish the facts. He bears witness: he is objective; he guarantees the clarity and purity of objects" (Haraway 1996, 4).

Boyle's treatise intrigues me not because it represents a scientific methodology, although his careful delineation of his scientific mode of analysis is engaging; rather, what draws me to Boyle's work is his attempt to explain scientifically the difference between white and Black. Boyle begins the treatise by asserting,

> When I applied myself to consider, how the cause of whiteness might be explained by intelligible and mechanical principles, I remembered not to have met with any things among the antient corpuscularian philosophers, touching the quality we call whiteness, save that Democritus is by Aristotle said to have ascribed the whiteness of bodies to their smoothness, and on the contrary their blackness to their asperity. (Boyle 1965/1772, 696–97)

In writing his account of the "experiment," Boyle states categorically that his aim is to prove that the cause of whiteness is that "white bodies reflect store of light" (699) and Black bodies do not. He describes experiment after experiment of what we know to be physics until experiment XI. This experiment stands out as something of an aberration in Boyle's essay. For, until this particular experiment, Boyle has largely confined his discussion to physical phenomena other than animals. In experiment XI, Boyle introduces for the first time the question of color in human beings and, in typical early modern English fashion, he does so by invoking the peoples of Africa as his "proof": "The cause of the blackness of those many nations, which by one common name we are wont to call Negroes, has been long since disputed of by learned men" (714). This dispute, Boyle contends, would have been resolved had these learned men "taken into consideration, why some whole races of other animals besides men, as foxes and hares, are distinguished by a blackness not familiar to the generality of animals of the same species" (714). In his experiment, Boyle seeks to satisfy himself in "matters of fact" as to the causality behind this phenomenon.

What is intriguing about Boyle's experiment is not his conclusions (which are generally consistent with other early modern discussions on Blackness) but the method he employs to arrive at his conclusions. Boyle states that it is his "present work to deliver rather matters historical than theories, [that he] shall annex some few of [his] collections, instead of a solemn disputation" (714). In an unusual departure from his normal manner of proceeding, this experiment does not follow the interrogative model he uses with the other experiments. In fact, this experiment might better be termed an explanation by "authority." What Boyle does in this section of his treatise is to summarize the different hypotheses which have been postulated over the centuries to explain Blackness in human beings. Like Thomas Browne, Boyle rejects prior theories (climatology, mythology, theology) and argues that the "principal cause (for which I would not exclude all concurrent ones) of the blackness of Negroes is some peculiar and seminal impression" (717). To support his argument of "seminal impression" Boyle (the scientist) draws upon what he terms the "testimony" of a countryman, Andrew Battel, "who being sent prisoner by the Portugals to Angola, lived there, and in the adjoining regions, partly as a prisoner, partly as a pilot, and partly as a soldier, near eighteen years" (718).

As if to further valorize Battel's legitimacy as a "modest witness," Boyle writes that the

same person as elsewhere a relation, which if I have made no use
at all of the liberty of a traveller, is very well worth our notice;
since this, together with that we have formerly mentioned of seminal impressions, shews a possibility, that a race of Negroes might
be begun, though none of the sons of Adam for many precedent
generations were of that complexion. For I see not, why it should
not be at least as possible, that white parents may sometimes have
black children, as that African Negroes should sometimes have
lastingly white ones; especially since concurrent causes may easily more befriend the productions of the former kind, than under
the scorching heat of Africa those of the latter. (Boyle 1965/1772,
719)

Despite his claim to deal only in what can be empirically proven, Boyle
ends up reproducing the same problematic paradigm as the learned men
he declares have gone awry as he uses arguments based on climate, geography, and myth to substantiate his suppositions and hypotheses.

Boyle ends his "experiment" by declaring that "it is high time for me to
dismiss observations, and go on with experiments" (719). A puzzled reader,
believing that what she read *was* an experiment, discovers that what
Boyle has in fact been about is not experimentation but observation —
that highly subjective, occasionally untrustworthy, and usually problematic mode of investigation. Anyone familiar with the body of writing produced in early modern European cultures concerned with explanations of
Blackness in human beings would not be surprised by the direction Boyle's
experiment took. What is noteworthy is that the scientist Boyle, when it
comes to treating color differences among humankind, disappears, to be
replaced by the Englishman Boyle. The organization and discussion of the
colors Black and white in Boyle's essay suggestively reproduce the subtle and problematic antithesis marked in George Best's explanation nearly
one hundred years earlier (see Hakluyt 1903/1600).

By the end of the seventeenth century, scientific investigation took up
the task of explaining the suppositions that Best and John Pory adum-
brated as they endeavored to grapple with the contradictions of existing
differences between human beings. In matters of human reproduction, it
was presumed that maleness and whiteness will always prevail — unless

there is a "wild seed." It is this anomaly that triggered writers, whether literary, philosophical, or ethnographic, to explore this anomaly — that nature or the imagination could, with a single act, negate the understood "truth" of presumably fixed natural categories. Through the publication of texts such as Boyle's treatise on color or Browne's *Pseudodoxica Epidemica*, as well as the many travel narratives, English culture was defining itself more and more in terms of colorism. As Kim F. Hall astutely surmises in her analysis of the powerful hold that Blackness, and its material body — the sub-Saharan African — had on the early modern English social, literary, and cultural imagination,

> descriptions of dark and light [or, more specifically, Black and white], rather than being mere indications of Elizabethan beauty standards or markers of moral categories, became in the early modern period the conduit through which the English began to formulate the notions of 'self' and 'other' so well known in Anglo-American racial discourses (Hall 1995, 2).

Early modern colonial enterprises engendered a new dynamic in gender and sexual relations, one shaped by an emerging concept of race based on colorism and physical appearance, which would come to define modern capitalism. Emerging concomitantly with this new gender dynamic is a growing anxiety over what was being produced in the sexual relations between Europeans and non-Europeans. In an attempt to explain rationally a puzzling situation — the fact that the offspring of a Black and white couple will not assume the color of the white partner — Best appears to set into motion what would become a general and pervasive anxiety about miscegenation. It is useful to reiterate in toto Best's anxiety-laden attempt to explain the perceived anomalies that derive from miscegenation:

> I my selfe have seene an Ethiopian as blacke as cole brought into England, who taking a faire English women to wife, begat a sonne in all respects as blacke as the father was, although England were his native countrey, and an English woman his mother.... And the most probable cause to my judgement is, that this blackeness proceedeth of some natural infection of the first inhabitants of that

Countrey, and so all the whole progenie of them descended, are still polluted with the same blot of infection ... by a lineall discent they have hitherto continued thus blacke. (Hakluyt 1903/ 1600, 262–63)

Best's language presupposes the superiority of whiteness and that in reproduction maleness and whiteness will always prevail unless there is some "natural" transgression. What goes unsaid however is that, with further miscegenation, Blackness can be effaced by whiteness, producing the white-presenting Clorindas.

The possibility, and likelihood, of the white Ethiopian is disturbing not because there is some fundamental difference between the Ethiopian and the English, but because it substantively proves that there is no difference beyond the superficial. It is this epistemological reality that makes white passing both problematic and desirable in a social order where the color of one's skin determines the condition of one's existence: whether an individual is enslaved or free, raped or honored, viewed as property or as human. If Blackness can disappear into whiteness, the white Ethiope becomes indistinguishable from the "white" English. Miscegenation makes porous the very core of Englishness, and its white supremacist thinking.

In this, I am reminded of Hayden White's argument in *Tropics of Discourse*, that although the forms of literature and history may at times differ, the rhetorical tropes deployed are the same (White 1978). If the function of the observer is to serve as "modest witness" to the experiment, then Best's narrative/authorial subject are indeed an exemplary "modest witness." More importantly, when we consider our own interpellated subjectivities, we cannot help but recognize that our own positions as "modest witnesses" to the *empirical truths of history* have been occasional acts of complicity in the perpetuation of discrete boundaries between "experience" and "knowledge." This is especially true in the case of the white-presenting, or white-passing, subject whose very presence points to the illogic of race and racism.

The real and hypothetical narratives of problematic whiteness, especially when produced by miscegenation, alluded to in the first "epigram" that opens this chapter are present throughout this chapter. The epigram is drawn from an unpublished fictionalized romance manuscript I wrote based on a "document of history" — the account of the "Negress Maria" taken by Francis Drake. In the manuscript, I posed a "what if" and fashioned a story of events that took place, in different ways, with different agents, in various configurations — all capable of producing a white-passing subject who might have been Aphra Behn. The imagined history which I have envisaged for Anne, the daughter of Elizabeth and Francisco Drake, whose rape and abduction by Francis Willoughby, Baron of Parham, mimics Francis Drake's rape and abduction of the Negress Maria, is a narrative whose genesis originates in the miscegenous space spawned by early modern English settler colonialism, the transatlantic slave trade, rape, and other forms of violence enacted against a people solely on the basis of skin color. And in the interstices of seventeenth-century English racism and settler colonialism, white passing inevitably leaves its traces.

Peopling an Island

In his introductory essay for the journal *Settler Colonial Studies*, Lorenzo Veracini outlines several key differences between colonialism and settler colonialism. According to Veracini, "colonialism is primarily defined by exogenous domination" and "thus has two fundamental and necessary components: an original displacement and unequal relations" (Veracini 2011, 1). While settler colonialism is an element of colonialism, "colonisers and settler colonisers want essentially different things" (1). As Veracini writes,

> in the case of colonial systems, a determination to exploit sustains a drive to sustain the permanent subordination of the colonized.... This permanence is not present under settler colonialism, which, on the contrary, is characterised by a persistent drive to ultimately supersede the conditions of its operation. The successful settler colonies "tame" a variety of wildernesses, end up establishing independent nations, effectively repress, co-opt, and extinguish indigenous alterities, and productively manage ethnic diversity. (2–3).

In essence, "colonialism reproduces itself and the freedom and equality of the colonised is forever postponed; settler colonialism, by contrast, extinguishes itself" (3). Settler colonialism's erasure of an indigenous presence rather than displacement is a key element in the process.

The erasure of indigenous peoples during the colonizing process requires, on the part of the colonizer, the racializing of both colonized and colonialist. The colonizer must also structure the interactions and representations of those interactions to justify the process. On the surface, Henry Neville's *The Isle of Pines* (2009/1668) may appear an odd text to add to a discussion of settler colonialism, colorism, and the romance genre. While Neville's text speaks to issues of colonialism, and settler colonialism specifically, an eyebrow or two might be raised at labeling *The Isle of Pines* a romance. The few scholars to write about Neville's text focus on the novella as a dystopian tale/allegory attached to the reign of Charles II and/or an engagement with patriarchal ideologies. For example, Amy Boesky writes, "*The Isle of Pines* allowed for the presentation of a new kind of utopia — one in which national identity is built out of the very act of interracial crossing established by the colony as most taboo" (Boesky 1995, 166). Will Stockton's reading, on the other hand, sees in the novella's conclusion, "the enforcement of monogamy" according to "Christian instruction," which effectively displaces the "endogamous and plural marriages in the island's implicitly Jewish past" (Stockton 2017, 106).

While Boesky and Stockton rightly draw attention to Neville's biblical framework and Boesky signals the English colonizing ambitions at the core of *The Isle of Pines*, neither approaches the white supremacist ideology at the core of the text. Moreover, the inattentiveness to the ways the narrative reinvents romance conventions to localize, contain, and erase potential threats to the privileging of whiteness and its dominance warrants greater scrutiny. In this chapter, I want to explore the ways white presenting threatens the ideology of white supremacy in *The Isle of Pines* and how romance conventions embody and embolden the ideology of settler colonialism at the heart of Neville's text.

The Isle of Pines, like so many early modern romance novels, frames itself in terms of history even as it recounts the fantastic. *The Isle of Pines Or, A Late Discovery of a Fourth ISLAND Near Terra Australis, Incognita* purports to be a "true relation of certain English persons, who in

Queen Elizabeths time, making a voyage to the East Indies were cast away, and wracked near the Coast of Terra Australis, Incognita, and all drowned, except one Man and four Women." (Neville 2009/1668, 189–90) The account is made "credible" by an English merchant's letter and several Dutch merchants as well. As the "author" writes, "this story seems very fabulous, yet the Letter is come to a known Merchant, and a from a good hand in France, so that I thought to fit to mention" (Neville 1668, A2v). The author's words evoke, as I have shown in Chapter One, the longstanding tension between "historiography" and "romance." We see a tone similar to the one in Georges de Scudery's preface to *Ibrahim, or the Illustrious Bassa*, where he declares what he considers to be the most significant: "but amongst all the rules which are to be observed in the compositions of these works, that of true resemblance is without question the most necessary; it is, as it were, the fundamental stone of this building" (de Scudery 1952/1674, 3). He then notes that, in his own work, he has "observed the Manners, Customs, Religions, and Inclinations of People: and to give a more true resemblance to things, I have made the foundations of my work Historical, my principal Personages such as are marked out in the true History for illustrious persons, and the wars effective" (4). Neville's use of the romance versus history trope is skillfully handled — by setting the story in an Elizabethan past he creates a romance context of historical believability.

The narrative of *The Isle of Pines* begins in 1569, when four English ships set sail for the East Indies to establish trade relations. On board were an English merchant, his wife, their son (twelve years old) and daughter (fourteen years of age), along with "two maidservants, one negro female slave, and" George Pine, "who went under him [the merchant] as a bookkeeper" (Neville 2009/1668, 194). As the ships sailed past Madagascar, a "violent storm" arose and all four ships were destroyed. Spying land, the captain and crew attempted to reach it but failed and lost their lives. Because George and the four women "could not swim" they were left behind on the ship and, as the ship broke on the rocks, the five miraculously survived when the "bowspright, which being broken off, was driven by the waves into a small creek" (195).

The five survivors find themselves on an uninhabited island and make shelter for the night using "some broken pieces of boards and planks, and some of the sails and rigging" (196). The next morning, they set about settling the island and in time, a domestic routine developed. After six months on the island, "idleness and a fullness of everything begot in [George] a desire for enjoying the women" (197). George states,

> Beginning now to grow more familiar, I had persuaded the two maids to let me lie with them, which I did at first in private; but after, custom taking away shame (there being none but us), we did it more openly, as our lusts gave us liberty. Afterwards my master's daughter was content also to do as we did. The truth is, they were all handsome women, when they had clothes, and well shaped, feeding well. For we wanted no food, and living idly, and seeing us at liberty to do our wills, without hope of ever returning home made us thus bold. One of my first consorts, with whom I first accompanied, the tallest and handsomest, proved presently with child. The second was my master's daughter. (198)

Without societal or patriarchal pressure to regulate their sexuality, especially female sexuality, George and the two maids give into their "lusts." In his description, George preens about not just his generative prowess (each woman quickly becoming pregnant) but the women's "handsome" looks.

Nowhere is the intersectionality of class, gender, *race*, and sexuality more thoroughly articulated than in George's account of how relations among the five survivors play out. His initial congress was with the maids whose class position was marginally closer to his own, perhaps a step below since he was a clerk. His dead master's daughter soon followed and, as we later learn, becomes favored not because she was the "handsomest" but because of her social class. The last woman to experience his sexual "prowess" was *his negro*. As George writes:

> The other also not long after fell into the same condition [pregnancy], none now remaining but my negro, who seeing what we did, longed also for her share. One night, I being asleep, my negro with the consent of the others got close to me, thinking it being dark to beguile me, but I awaking and feeling her, and perceiving who it was, yet willing to try the *difference*, satisfied myself with

her, as well as with one of the rest. That night, although the first time, she proved also with child, so that in the year of our being there, all my women were with child by me; and they all coming at different seasons, were a great help to one another. (198, emphasis added)

The four women — the merchant's daughter, the two English maidservants, and the "negro female slave" — in effect became George's harem.

George's sexual relations with the four women (three of whom he "married" or called "wife") continued until their deaths. The women's extraordinary fertility gave George forty-seven children (most of whom were girls), all of whom survived: "We had no clothes for them, and therefore when they had sucked, we laid them in the moss to sleep, and took no further care of them; for we knew, when they were gone more would come; the women never failing once a year at least. And none of the children, for all the hardship we put them to, were ever sick" (198). As the children grew into maturity, especially sexual, George "mated" his daughters and sons. With his grandchildren and his great-grandchildren, he was more careful in arranging "marriages" based on an adherence to the idea of consanguinity: "I took off the males of one family, and married them to the females of another, not letting any to marry their sisters, as we did formerly out of necessity" (199).

"Miscegenation and orgiastic sexual indulgence are thus added to the list of the taboos broken by the text," Susan Bruce observes, and "in the remainder of Pine's narrative incest quietly joins this catalogue of transgressions, since Pine's children must sleep with their half-siblings to produce their own issue" (Bruce 2009, xxxviii). Finally, nearing his eightieth year and adhering to the laws of primogeniture, George gave his "cabin and furniture that was left, to [his] eldest son (after [his] decease), who had married [his] eldest daughter by [his] beloved wife" and named this son "King and Governor of all the rest" (Neville 2009/1668, 199). He then "informed them of the manners of Europe, and charged them to remember the Christian religion, after the manner of them that spake the same language, and to admit no other" (199), including instructions about regulating the Pines' sexuality.

Having arranged for the succession, George summoned his other descendants, who numbered 1789 and gave them his blessing. It is not until the end of his narrative that George names himself and the women:

> I gave this people, descended from me, the name of the English Pines, George Pine being my name, and my master's daughter's name Sarah English. My two other wives were Mary Sparkes, and Elizabeth Trevor. So their several descendants are called the English, the Trevors, and the Phils, from the Christian name of the negro, which was Philippa, she having no surname; and the general name of the whole the English Pines (200).

I want to focus on the significance of George's words at the end of his narrative. First, although all of his offspring are "white in color," he is careful to articulate class and lineal distinctions. Within traditional patriarchy, the offspring carried the name of the father. In this new space, such conformity runs counter to the articulation of an atypical social and racial hierarchy. While the group as a whole are called Pine, the offspring of each woman carry the mother's last name. Phillipa's lack of a surname is inextricably tied to her status as enslaved — a point George makes clear through his use of the possessive to mark her subjectivity. Furthermore, whenever he speaks of Phillipa it is generally with reference to her designation as a "negro": "the negro had no pain at all" or "not with the black at all after she was with child," or "my negro" or the "Negro-woman." By refusing to name Phillipa as a wife, as he does with the other women, George ensures that her Blackness codes her as little more than a means of sexual gratification and reproduction.

During the first year on the island, four children are born, one boy and three girls. What immediately sets Philippa's daughter apart is that she is described as "a fine white girl" despite being the child of "one of the handsomest blacks [George] had seen" (198). As it turns out, all of Philippa's children are born white and "as comely as any of the rest" (198). Yet, as the narrative continues, these white-presenting children remain constitutively identified as "Black": "the negro twelve" or "the Phils, from the Christian name of the negro." This "Blackness" becomes most firmly entrenched in the reader's imagination when the present-day "King" and

"Governor" of the island, William Pine (a descendant of George Pine and Sarah English), describes several insurrections to his Dutch visitors. A segment of the "English Pines" have fallen into "whoredoms, incests, and adultery; so that what my grandfather was forced to do for necessity, they did for wantonness," William reports (201). His father, George's son, "assembled all the country near unto him" and, armed, they "marched against the 'wicked ones', [who fled] fearing their deserved punishment" (202).

It should come as no surprise that the "greatest offender" proved to be the "second son of the Negro-woman that came with George into this island" (202). Judged guilty of "divers ravishings and tyrannies," John Phill was executed. This account would not be problematic were it not for an another attempted insurrection by Henry Phill, the "chief ruler of the tribe or family of the Phills, being the offspring of George Pines which he had by the negro-woman" (207). Despite their whiteness, the Phills are morally "conditioned" by their ancestress Phillipa's Blackness. Similar to the whiteness of Charikliea and Clorinda, the Phills' white skin bespeaks a promise of assimilation. However, for white supremacy to work, the "properties" that mark Blackness as inferior must be made visible. Just as Fairfax/Tasso before him, Neville does this by localizing "Blackness" as interiorized and thus an inheritable biological trait that manifests in behavior. In effect, while they may not have inherited Phillipa's skin color, the Phils did inherit her "bad blood" in the form of "sexual aggression and subversion" (Boesky 1995).

The anxiety that rumbles beneath the surface of *The Isle of Pines* is that there is nothing to distinguish the Pines except for their surnames since the island's entire population is white. To sustain the superiority of whiteness and capitalize on English racism's anti-Blackness that enables Neville's romance, the white-passing "negro" must be exposed. In other words, for "whiteness" to retain its status of superiority, "Blackness" must retain its negativity even when that "Blackness" is contained in a "white" body. It is this racecraft that surfaces in the representation of the Phils as licentious, violent, and uncivilized, and what constitutes them as white-passing "negroes." Boesky rightly argues that "George Pine has authored [the Phils], and they are trapped inside his representation, a representation that simultaneously separates them as a 'race' and renders them subordinate" (Boesky 1995, 180). In essence, and I shall return to this point below, the Phils become the "natives" who must be subjugated and eventually erased from the colonized land despite their whiteness.

A Settler Colonialist's Dream

One of the questions that puzzled me on my first reading of *The Isle of Pines* was the author's decision to precisely date the story. That is, rather than offer his readers an ambiguous timeframe during the reign of Elizabeth I, Neville begins his account with a precise date, 1589. The 1580s were significant years in English colonialist endeavors. In 1584, Walter Raleigh obtained his patent for the colonization of Virginia, while the defeat of the Spanish navy ships in 1588 ensured England's ability to further its colonial aims. This period was also marked by cartographic explorations, finding new lands and exploring uncharted regions. At the time Neville wrote *The Isle of Pines*, England had established colonies in the Caribbean and the Americas, and the discovery of new or uncharted lands had waned. Yet the novella hearkens back to a moment of the newness of geographic discovery. In what follows, I want to discuss the novella's idealization of settler colonialism as part of its political logic. While I am not arguing against readings based on Neville's political beliefs, I am suggesting that the novella does more than take allegorical potshots at Charles II and his court. *The Isle of Pines* is a text that figures the unsettling prospect of unchecked miscegenation, and its societal consequences, on settler colonialism and attempts to resolve the problem within the romance structure.

A presumption at work in the novella is the idea of unpopulated spaces in the world. The discovery of land devoid of people is, in many ways, a colonizing dream, especially as early modern English travel narratives increasingly debunked that idea. Thus, what makes Neville's text such a fascinating settler colonialist narrative is that he engages in world-building from scratch — yet, to make the romance of settler colonialism work, he needs to "people" the land. Hence the characters of George Pine and the four women who were part of an English mercantile group sailing to "East India" to "settle a factory for the advantage of Trade" (Bruce 2009, 194). George was employed as a Factor's bookkeeper and, when a fierce storm claims the lives of the captain, the ship's crew, the Factor, his wife, son, and everyone else on board the merchant ship, George and the four women are the only survivors. Ironically, they survived because they couldn't swim and had remained on board the ship (195). Once on land, George starts a fire for the women and then goes off to find survivors: "I hooted, and made all the noise I could; neither could I perceive the foot-steps of any living Creature (save a few Birds, and other Fowls)" (195).

After creating a shelter for himself and the women, George states he and the white women "slept soundly" while "the Blackmoor being less sensible than the rest we made our Centry" (195). As Boesky argues, Phillipa's position on the island is never ambiguated: she is a servant there "to safeguard the whites from the wildness they dread" (Boesky 1995, 173). As he explores "the large island," George discovers that it is isolated, "out of sight of any other Land," and "wholly uninhabited by any people" (197). From this moment, the island becomes not just a temporary refuge until rescue land, but land to be settled: "And having now no thought of ever returning home, as having resolved and sworn each to other, never to part or leave one another, or the place" (199). In writing the island as "unin-habited," Neville performs an a priori disappearance of natives to set into motion the creation of a settler colony. This "authorial" erasure forestalls questions about indigenous sovereignty of the island, the need to "man-age and neutralize indigenous difference," or domination (Veracini 2011, 8). In other words, there are no "they" who have "to go away" (9). What *The Isle of Pines* romances is an ability to engage in settler colonialism without the hazards that come with pre-existing occupancy. In other words, there are no indigenous bodies to engage as equals nor any need for "recogni-tion and reconciliation." Importantly, "one of the necessary prerequisites of colonialism … the original demands for labour and thus for indigenous disappearance must also cease" (Veracini 2011, 8).

The obvious absence of the "native" or indigenous potential to satisfy this prerequisite of colonialism has to be addressed. This absence, as Neville's romance illustrates, requires a necessary force of labor if the set-tler colonial project is to come to fruition. *The Isle of Pines* is written and published at a particular juncture in English cultural and economic history. The nation's colonies, especially in the Americas, are beginning to flourish and represent a potentially significant share of the domestic commodity market. The English increasingly controlled the transatlantic slave trade to its colonies, a factor which heightens the interactions between English and African in unprecedented ways, especially with respect to the African maternal body (Morgan 2018). The African presence in late seventeenth-century England is far more visible than ever before, and no less troubling for the construction of a homogeneous "whiteness" for English society. It is this presence, I would argue, that serves Neville's "imaginary need" for a native presence that also needs to be absent.

The romance genre remained a stable and popular means for the elucidation of this particular strand of white supremacy idealized in a fantasy that "aims at the transfiguration of the world of everyday life in such a way as to restore the conditions of some lost Eden" (Jameson 1981, 110). Neville's *The Isle of Pines*, for all its troubling sexism and racism, makes this point most obviously. By making all the Pines "white," Neville simultaneously deflates once and for all the notion of race as an inflexible dichotomy. On the contrary, the romancing of white supremacy required the parameters of race to be calibrated along an entirely different spectrum that took into account the possibility of white passing.

In this the Phils speak to pre- and early modern English ambivalence towards the white-presenting Black subject capable of white passing. Like both Charikliea and Clorinda, the Phils bear the imprimatur of parental Blackness. What distinguishes these white-presenting chracterizations from each other is the ways in which they are assimilable into the functionality of English racism. Because Heliodorus's culture had not yet made color an absolute marker in the definition of racial identity, Charikliea's whiteness is less important than her identity as a princess. Fairfax/Tasso's Clorinda, on the other hand, bespeaks an intermediary moment in the recalibration of race. Clorinda's whiteness is problematic because it conceals her true identity, Ethiopian, even as serves as a sign, at her death, of her membership in the Christian community. What the Phils indicate is the perception that, even if desired, the "white Ethiopian" cannot be assimilated into the dominant culture because their Blackness will always work to manifest itself. However, what *The Isle of Pines* cannot suppress, try as it might, is the fact there are Phils who do succeed in white passing and are invisible Black bodies moving freely among the whiteness that is England.

Like many of the fictional narratives emerging in the wake of the enslavement and transportation of Black Africans to the Americas, Neville's text contributes to a cultural discourse that Blackness will inevitably expose itself. *The Isle of Pines* rehearses a familiar romance trope of racialization in the descriptions of the problematic behavior of the Phils. From the outset, Phillipa's status as an enslaved Black woman and thus inferior becomes a genetic trait each of her descendants will carry. What are we to make of Neville's "colorism" — where the offspring and descendants of an African Black woman inherit their father's skin color? Where the only markers inherited from their maternal side are behavioral? It is this piece that is often overlooked in critical studies of *The Isle of Pines*. After Philippa's death, there are no visibly "Black" people on the island. The only way to romanticize her Blackness is to internalize it, to make it a behavioral factor, not a somatic one, and to position those labeled "Black" as a problem of villainous indigeneity.

My reading of Neville's text as an early modern "romance novella" centers settler colonialism and white supremacy as historical narratives rather than a "utopian" or political allegory. I want to suggest that *The Isle of Pines* enacts the model of a romance even if the text handles the usual romance tropes or conventions differently than its predecessors. There is the heroic figure of George Pine who achieves an unusual (polyamorous) happily ever after. While initial obstacles are natural and a matter of survival, once the island is "peopled," the trope of human villainy becomes the source of conflict, internal and external. Ultimately, Neville's text works as romance fiction because it offers a "more true resemblance to things" that renders the "fantasy" acceptable to readers. Simply put, the success of the romance novel has long inhered in the author's ability to make a fantastical narrative believable and the best way, as de Scudery notes, is to lay a foundation in the "historical" (de Scudery 1952/1674, 4). History, in *The Isle of Pines*, however, is bracketed. Despite the inclusion of a late seventeenth-century preface that documents the "discovery of the island and its natives," and the transmission of that knowledge by means of a Dutch merchant's eye-witness account and William Pine's letters, the narrative itself is set in a "past" impossible to evidentiarily recuperate except through what is printed in the text.

That past is entwined with racial capitalism and African women's reproductive lives. The violence perpetrated against the Phils acknowledges a
failure on the part of George Pine to restructure the patriarchal, and I
would argue the legal, structure of governance on the island with respect
to Black bodies. As Jennifer L. Morgan explains in a discussion of the 1662
Virginia code that shifted hereditary status of children fathered by white
men:

> If a child fathered by a free white man with an enslaved African
> woman became a slave, that child was transformed from kin to
> property. Thus, in essence, slaveowners and slaveowning legis-
> lators enacted the legal and material substitution of a thing for
> a child: no white man's *child* could be enslaved, while all black
> women's *issue* could. This happens as though it were common
> sense, when, in fact, it was a profound reversal of European
> notions of heredity in the service of a relatively new notion of dif-
> ference and bondage. (Morgan 2018, 3, original emphases)

By upholding patriarchal lines of descent (child inherits the status of the
father), George's children with Phillipa shared the same freedoms as their
siblings despite maternal status. While Phillipa is never called a "slave,"
George's descriptive language — black, negro, negro-servant — estab-
lishes clear a distinction between her and the other servants.

The establishment of separate communities on the island does not
change the hierarchal and social relations produced as a matter of settler
colonialism. If anything, as the narrative illustrates, the social, political,
and racializing hierarchies George Pine brings with him from England
remain intact. Even so, *The Isle of Pines* fundamentally shifts the white
supremacy narrative in unexpected directions. We cannot help but follow
the unspoken ideological path the romance lays before us. We are forced
to ask, Is race real? Is it constructed? Is it an "as-if" concept, something we
all agree to bestow on each other? Is it a relational concept, existing only
in binary fashion (e.g., Black/white), so that if all the people on a tropi-
cal island, say, looked pretty much the same, there would be no race or
races? Contemporary science, despite eugenics clinger-ons, tells us that
whites and Blacks have more genes in common than the ones that distin-

guish them, and the variability between the average white and the average Black, in genetic makeup and physical appearance, is less than the variability within each group. What then, does it mean to be white, or of any other race, for that matter? While the laws of genetics would have eventually rendered Philippa's descendants "white" (possibly by the third and definitely by the fourth generation), Neville's failure to represent Philippa's firstborn child as a mixed race or "mulatta" opens a Pandora's box that proves difficult to shut.

To conclude, it seems fitting to cite Toni Morrison's observation that

> images of impenetrable whiteness need contextualizing to explain their extraordinary power, pattern, and consistency. Because they appear almost always in conjunction with representations of black or Africanist people who are dead, impotent, or under complete control, these images of blinding whiteness seem to function as both antidote for and meditation on the shadow that is companion to this whiteness — a dark and abiding presence that moves the hearts and texts of American literature with fear and longing. (Morrison 1992, 33)

What *The Isle of Pines* illustrates, in the end, is that the ideology of racial colorism is as unstable as the romance genre. When faced with a "white Ethiopian" or a "white Negro," how do you insist on adherence to their "assigned" racial identity? How do you regulate a person whose biophysical lineage reflects a Black and a white ancestor but whose own physical appearance is white? At what point does the individual's relationship to Blackness and whiteness become unintelligible in the context of older narratives of colorism and need to be interrogated in some other manner? Finally, at what point does, or can, colorism as a by-product of English racism and white supremacy cease to matter?

Chapter Four

Seeing What You Want

> What *is it* about passing that lets it live so large and so
> long in the public imagination? Passing — both as literary
> trope and as lived experience — seems to have such an
> unlikely and extended historical and literary shelf life.
> (Elam 2018, 241, original emphasis)

> People often times see what you want them to see.
> (Galen Vachon [Jenkins 1996, 287])

Romance author Beverly Jenkins was not the first Black American author
to make the romance genre her preferred mode of writing. When she
penned *Night Song* (1994) Jenkins joined a small yet growing number of
Black women writers (Sandra Kitt, Elsie Washington, writing behind the
pseudonym Rosalind Welles, and Francis Ray, to name a few). Most often
categorized as "African American fiction," Black romance until recently has
been a neglected area of scholarly research. Whether intentional or not,
the collapsing of romance into African American fiction does a diservice to
the abovementioned authors' careers and canon. Of these writers, Jenkins
was the only one to focus her writing in the area of historical romance,
although over the course of her career, she has moved freely between
the historical and contemporary romance subgenres. For the purpose of
this chapter, I define historical romance as a subset of the romance genre
set prior to the twentieth century. Most of Jenkins's novels take place
between 1850 and 1900. While all of her romance fiction centers Black love
and Black communities, two of her historical novels engage the themes of
Race and Romance: Coloring the Past: *Indigo* (1996) and *Forbidden* (2016),
and, as I hope to illustrate, foreground the troubling nature of colorism
and the unspoken illogic that sits at the heart of white supremacy.

If, as early modern romance theorists argue, "amongst all the rules
which are to be observed in the compositions of these works [romances],
that of true resemblance is without question the most necessary; it is, as

it were, the fundamental stone of this building" (de Scudery 1952/1674, 3), then Jenkins's historical romances definitely adhere to this generic tenet. Jenkins is meticulous in her research on the histories of enslaved peoples, the emergence of Black communities post–Civil War in the United States, and the work of racism and sexism involved in the settler colonialism of indigenous lands in what came to be the United States. The result of Jenkins's attention to history is often a scholarly undervaluing of the literary and romance conventions at work. In other words, the political, social, and economic world-building she does can obscure the romance fiction that, in my opinion, places her alongside the early modern authors I've been discussing. The world of her historical romances disrupts readerly expectations about Black people and Black romance. As Jenkins observes, publishers and readers seem to believe "when you write a 19th-century story, featuring Black people, it should center on slavery. So here I come with this story [Night Song], 19th-century Black people living in a small town on the plains of Kansas" (Moody-Freeman 2020).

In ways similar to Heliodorus's Aethiopica, Jenkins's historical romances offer readers the unexpected, moving them into a world both historical and imaginative to explore questions of love, identity, virtues, and beauty with a Black couple at the heart of the romance narrative. I focus on Forbidden and, to a lesser degree, Indigo, because the anxiety evident in the racecraft at work in the romances of Heliodorus, Fairfax/Tasso, and Neville is laid bare in Jenkins's romance novels. White-presenting subjectivites created an unfathomable racial anxiety for English culture especially in the lands subject to its settler colonialist agenda. In these spaces, the non-white body needed to be erased and or policed. Nowhere is this more evident than in the settler-colonialist United States where the enslavement of African peoples fed a white supremacist ideology that continues to plague the nation. While legal and political institutions sanctioned efforts to police Black and white bodies from the inception of English settler colonialism, a history of rape and miscegenation points to the failure of such efforts. Thus, it isn't surprising that white passing routinely surfaced as a cultural fear in the United States. In ways that acknowledge this fear and the inability to regulate white passing, what Forbidden and Indigo both illustrate is the impossibility of white supremacy to sustain its racial logic. Where white supremacist logic argues that race and its associated colorism are immutable, Jenkins's novels demonstrate that somatic and physiologically-based notions are illogical, which allows race to become a performative act.

Performing Whiteness

At the end of *Aethiopika*, Charikliea is recognized as the daughter of the Ethiopian King, the union between her and Theagenes is sanctioned, and her right to inherit the Ethiopian throne is secure. Patrilineal doubts were put to rest by a simple birthmark that established her Blackness. Because of this narrative detail, *Aethiopika* contributes to and participates in the idea that "race will tell out" — something we see in the adaptations of the romance. In essence, Blackness, no matter how deeply buried in whiteness, will eventually surface to mark a person's racial identity. *The Isle of Pines* demonstrably shows the continuation of this point of view; although the Phils are as white-skinned as the Trevors, Sparks, and Pines, their inherited Blackness surfaces in their behavior (considered inheritable traits from their Black ancestress Phillipa). It is worth it at this point to invoke the 1662 Virginia statute that not only redefined an enslaved person's patrilineal status but, as Jennifer L. Morgan argues, "systematically alienated the enslaved from their kin and their lineage" (Morgan, 2018, 1). The law read:

> Whereas some doubts have arisen whether children got by any Englishman upon a negro woman shall be slave or free, Be it therefore enacted and declared by this present grand assembly, that all children borne in this country shall be held bond or free only according to the condition of the mother — Partus Sequitur Ventrem. And that if any Christian shall commit fornication with a negro man or woman, hee or shee soe offending shall pay double the fines imposed by the former act. (Laws of Virginia, 1662 Act XII; Latin added by William Henig, *The Statutes at Large*, 1819, quoted in Morgan 2018, 1)

For two hundred years, this law and its variations by other states was used not only to sustain the practice of enslavement but also to justify white supremacy's violent control over enslaved women's reproduction and any children born as a result of that enslavement. By putting "into code the assumptions about racial inheritance" (Morgan 2018, 3). Virginia and the United States made explicit what had long rumbled beneath the ideology of race in early modern English culture: while it was possible to regulate somatically visible Blackness, it was nearly impossible to regulate somatically invisible Blackness.

It is this context that informs the storyline of Rhine Fontaine, the white-passing hero of Jenkins's *Forbidden*. In 1865, Union soldier Rhine Fontaine returns to the planation where he had been born, the offspring of the white plantation owner and "the descendant of an enslaved African queen" (Jenkins, 2016, 6). Seeking information about his sister, Rhine heads to the slave cabins only to find the enslaved had fled and the one person remaining was his father's wife, Sally Ann Fontaine. The woman's bitterness and hatred doesn't stop her from giving him what little information she possesses. As he is about to leave, Sally Ann asks, "[w]hat are you doing in a fancy Yankee uniform?" When Rhine remains silent, she says, "Passing again, are you?" (6).

Rhine's lack of an answer speaks volumes for the direction of the novel, as is Jenkins's description: "Rhine's ivory skin, jet black hair, and green eyes made it easy for him to pass as someone he wasn't. He was ten years old when he first realized he could do it successfully" (7). Sally Ann's words evoke a painful memory of being beaten until "he bled." Yet, during the entire scene, Rhine remains silent. In a striking moment, Jenkins gives Sally Ann the final words: "Andre turns his back on his race, and you turn back on yours. What a wretched pair you are" (7). Having received information about his sister, Rhine departs, trusting that the old African queens whose blood ran in his veins would reunite him with Sable in the near future. With that belief settled firmly in his heart, he heads to his own future — one he planned to live out as "White" (7). At this point (prologue), the reader and Rhine are the only ones aware of his decision.

The word "pass" has a curious and complex socio-lexical history in Anglo-American culture. As defined by *Webster's International Dictionary*, "pass" is, "to move or be transferred from one place, state, or condition to another; to change possession, condition or circumstances, to undergo transition or conversion." In both noun and verb forms, "pass" has also come to signify death. Instead of using dead or died, people often substitute a verbal phrase such as "he passed away" or "he passed on" or, simply, "he passed," or "his passing was unexpected." The type of "passing" that is suggested in Weever's epigram in Chapter Two, which is the theoretical concern of this study, is rooted in all these definitions and yet distinctive in its own right. This passing marks the process whereby a person self-consciously enters into an identity made possible by the instability and uninhabitability of the very ideologies created to prevent such entries. Once entering into this identity, however, the passer must maintain the boundaries of this identity, vigilantly guarding against the slippages, erasures, and exposures which once defined them in terms of another identity. The objective is never to be found out. Modes of passing, whether gender, class, or color, occur in a symbolic economy predicated upon violation of social, political, and juridical norms. Such acts constitute what can be defined as the self-consciously "performative enactment" of social norms, "performative" here having both its theatrical connotation and the reiterative denotation that Judith Butler ascribes to the term (Butler 1993).

To argue that race is performative is to insist on the rejection of the idea that race is constitutively defined in terms of perceptible biological differences: epidermal coloring, hair texture, the shape and size of the body, and other physiological attributes. In addition, a long list of cultural and social behavior have morphed into quasi-biological predicates of race — sexuality, intellect, and morality. Yet, for obvious and complex historical reasons, it is difficult to envision a theoretical discussion of race that does so without resorting to an analysis dependent on the physical appearance of the body that is "racialized." Even more to the point, it is nearly impossible to treat race in terms other than skin color and as a racializing predicate ideologically ingrained in the collective cultural consciousness of European societies since the Middle Ages. If, as I am suggesting, we view race as a "performative act," then we need to examine more carefully the ways in which transgressive racial identity, the "color-passing" subject, functions as a "corporeal field of cultural play" that "compe[ls] [us] to live in a world in which [races] constitute univocal signifiers, in which [race] is stabilized, polarized, rendered discrete and intractable" (In recasting Butler's observations on gender, I've substituted "race" for "gender." Butler 1988, 528).

As Julia Thomas observes, "Our eyes are not simple recorders or receptacles of information: they do not simply mirror a world that exists unproblematically outside them" (Thomas 2001, 4). In fact, she continues,

> Perception involves not just the act of looking but decision-making too: the brain searches for the best possible interpretation of the available data. And this idea of 'interpretation' is of more than passing significance because in order for the brain to transform what is seen into something recognisable, to create meanings through sight, it relies on learnt assumptions about the characteristics of, and differences between, things. Such distinctions, however natural they seem, are not inherent in sight or even in the visualized world. (4)

Furthermore, Thomas argues, "It is more than biology that dictates how one sees. Seeing is bound up in value judgements (one assesses things by their appearance) and, because it is spatially and temporally limited (one cannot see everything simultaneously but only a certain amount and at any one moment), it involves an element of choice" (4).

White passing arises as the cultural and ideological interlocutor of a concept that insists upon sight as the infallible medium of recognition and knowledge. Generally, one person sees another person and, based upon their physical appearance (systemized value judgments), immediately decides how or whether to categorize their (choice). Of course, this system works well if one can be certain that the interpretation of what one is seeing is valid. For example, a man racially designated as "white" sees a woman whose skin color is dark brown. The man racially categorized "white" draws upon a received body of cultural and linguistic codes designed to aid his interpretation of what he sees: assumptions about color, physiognomy, culture, status, and hierarchy, as well as a cultural lexicon to name what he is about to interpret. As a result, the man "sees" the woman as a "Black" woman, and thus racially different and possibly inferior. Conversely, if the woman "seen" has "white" skin, then the man undergoes the same reasoning process but reaches a different conclusion.

The epistemological problem, I would argue, is extant in the second scenario. Here, we need to recognize that the "white" man may be "reading" the woman's body both correctly and incorrectly; incorrectly in that the woman was born to parents of African ancestry and correctly because her physical appearance marks her as "white." If there are no other signs to indicate the woman's lineal "Blackness," the man does not question what he "sees." Moreover, should the woman be joined by two "Black" individuals and she acknowledges a kinship or group relation, or if through some other means the man discovers his mis-reading, then he must question not only the relationship between seeing and knowledge, but also the belief system that constitutes the way in which he interprets what he sees. Finally, should the man remain ignorant of the woman's genealogy, and the woman is aware of his mis-reading and she does not correct his assumption about her racial identity, then her action constitutes deliberate white passing. As Amy Robinson argues, "[i]f the action of sight requires a subject, then *intuition* summons a denotation of unmediated access to a truth whose function is the fortification of the subject who looks. It is thus no accident that the eyes are named as the privileged vehicle of intuitive knowledge" (Robinson 1994, 720-21, original emphasis). What intuition enables is the "visibility of the apparatus of passing — literally the machinery that enables the performance. What the "in-group" sees is not a stable prepassing identity but rather the apparatus of passing that manufactures presumption (of heterosexuality, of whiteness) as the means to a successful performance" (721–22).

Forbidden is a novel about this variation of passing since several members of the Black community "suspect" Rhine's performance. Rhine deliberately misrepresents his matrilineal heritage, the one that gives him his "Blackness," although he never allows himself to "forget" his ancestral "Queens." When we encounter Rhine five years later, he is a wealthy, prosperous businessman living in Virginia City, Nevada and the fact that he is white passing is neither known nor seems to trouble Rhine in ways often depicted in African American literature that features passing narratives. For Rhine, the decision made at the age of ten has borne unexpected fruit not just for him but for his "race" as well. In other words, Jenkins does not cast her romance hero as "the tragic mulatto," which stems as much from an unwillingness to write "Black trauma porn" as from her research *and* her authorial awareness of the possibilities of romance (Moody-Freeman 2020). In this, *Forbidden* is more akin to pre- and early modern romances than the passing narratives of the nineteenth and early twentieth centuries. In most passing novels, the white-passing subject experiences a sense of guilt about what is viewed by both Black and white people as a duplicitous act. Strikingly, this "guilt" is absent in Rhine. What seems to emerge in the novel for Rhine is regret. Regret that "by passing, he'd gained a lot in terms of wealth and prestige," but "he'd [also] lost a lot," especially his ability to "participate fully because he was no longer a member of the race" (Jenkins 2016, 105).

When his brother Andrew advises Rhine to "find you someone to love and live out your old age in contentment as I plan to do" (102), Rhine's response is a simple, "I need to help, Drew" (102). Andrew's reply speaks to the bond between the brothers despite the genesis of that bond: "There are other men helping in their own way. Leave it to them. I don't want you lynched or beaten to death" (102). Andrew's worry doesn't deter Rhine who believed himself "uniquely qualified to be a voice for those who did care, because of his passion, education, and ability to pass for White. He may have turned his back on being Black, but not on his race" (103). From its inception in 1865, Rhine's passing has been personal and political. His relationship with his brother brought him education and wealth, both of which Rhine used to advantage his "race." What is provocative in Jenkins words, "He may have turned his back on being Black, but not his race," is the suggestion that Blackness is not race. As I have argued elsewhere, race is a "shaping fantasy" (Hendricks 1996) and Rhine's performance is indicative of that fact. In Rhine, we witness "the performative dimension of racial formation" (Elam 2018, 245). In fact, Michele Elam contends, this "is not to suggest race is play without social consequence or that such a theorization evades the everyday of racism (both common canards); quite the contrary, the performance of passing can often best index the truth of the lie of race" (245).

Until the day he rescues Eddy Carmichael in an unforgiving desert, Rhine does not seem to question the decision he made five years prior. He considers the benefits to the Black community to be worth the sacrifice. Eddy, however, proves to be an unexpected challenge. As Eddy lies in his bed, recuperating from near fatal sun exposure, Jenkins describes Rhine's reaction:

> Rhine surveyed his sleeping guest. He ran his eyes over the clear-as-glass ebony skin, the long sweep of her lashes, and her perfect mouth. While in the tub, she'd taken him by surprise when she opened her eyes, looked deeply into his own, and cupped his cheek as if they'd been lovers. The urge to turn her hand and place his lips against her damp palm had also taken him by surprise. He had a fiancée and was due to be married before year's end. He had no business thinking about kissing another woman. (Jenkins 2016, 40–41)

What is significant about the final sentence is the absence of "white" self-consciousness about Rhine's desire for Eddy. I want to suggest that this moment is Jenkins's subtle reminder that Rhine belongs to the same racial group as Eddy. Ironically, throughout much of the novel, it is Eddy who foregrounds Rhine's "whiteness" and therefore the impossibility of their growing attraction turning into a relationship: "Eddy had no experience with men, but there was something in his gaze that gave her pause. He was without a doubt the handsomest man she'd ever met, but she knew a man of his race and wealth wouldn't be interested in a near destitute Colored woman, at least not legitimately" (54). The relationship between Rhine and Eddy builds in a familiar Jenkins's style — a passionate slow burn. By the end of the first third of the novel, Rhine knows exactly what he wants. The choice he has to make has consequences that affect more than just him.

Rhine and Eddy dance around their deepening attraction to each other, although it is clear that it is a wasted effort. Eddy, believing Rhine is white, has the most difficult time dealing with her feelings: "... instead of leaving he stood there silently, just as he had last night, his gaze holding hers, and the sensations shimmering over her were getting harder and harder to ignore" (68). When a date with Zeke Reynolds (the town's Black carpenter) reveals the depths of Eddy's conflicted emotions about Rhine, she confesses to Sylvie, "How can I possibly want to be with someone I know is forbidden and will probably break my heart?" (270). Later, while Eddy waits for Jim to arrive, Sylvie asks only one question: "Are you sure this is what you want to do?" (285). Eddy's reply is a single word, "yes."

That single word, "yes," is imbued with more than emotional weight. Eddy hasn't just consented to dinner with Rhine. She has also opened the possibility for a relationship, whether she admits it to herself or not: "Sylvie smiled. 'No honey, but you'll have to be discreet — both of you will.'" Eddy's reply, "'We're only going to have dinner this one time,'" rings hollow to Sylvie, the novel's readers, and to Eddy (285). The dinner and its aftermath leaves Eddy even more emotionally complicated, especially after Rhine's marriage proposal. When she realizes he is serious, she chooses "her words carefully" and says, "You know what we'd be facing. It might look to be an easy road from where you sit, but it isn't. You're not Colored and I'm not White. Us being together is against the law almost everywhere" (295). Rhine's confession, "But I'm not White either," earns a chuckle. Eddy assumes that his words were a reflection of "all the good she was told he'd done on behalf of the city's Colored community," and says, "Maybe not inside" (295).

At Rhine's "Not outside either," Eddy's reason takes hold and she realizes what he is admitting. Jenkins reveals Rhine's white passing simply, saying, "I'd like to tell you a story." It is in this chapter we learn the full extent of Rhine's life since the war ended — his birth, the reunion with his brother Andrew, the acquisition of his wealth (Andrew "gave me half that stack of winnings"), and Rhine's decision to settle in Virginia City. As Rhine recounts, "When we left St. Louis, I came to Virginia City, bought stock in the mines, made myself even more wealthy. He [Andrew] went on to San Francisco, invested his money, made himself even more wealthy, too, and now he's a banker" (297). The more Eddy learns about Rhine, the more she understands yet she cannot refrain from asking the question, "Why didn't you change your name? Don't most people who pass do that?" (297). Rhine tells her he wanted his sister Sable "to be able to find [him]."

In everything he has done since he chose to perform whiteness, Rhine's actions have been driven by love — love for his sister, for his "race," and for the "Old Queens." It is obvious that Rhine's white passing proved beneficial except to his ability to marry for love. His engagement to Natalie Greer was a pragmatic decision, one based on political aspirations, not love. Rhine's decision to end the engagement, Jenkins makes clear, is born of his love for Eddy and the recognition that he no longer wants to live as a passing subject. Once he makes the decision to reveal his racial heritage, he is determined to protect Eddy and the Black community of Virginia City. Rhine sends a coded message to his brother Andrew with the news that he's "had a change of heart." He reassures Eddy "his business holdings and money won't be affected" since "it isn't against Nevada law for me to own land or a business" (298). Eddy understands that behind the words is something far greater than a mere "change of heart." Her joy at becoming Rhine's wife is muted by what his revelation means:

> The next few weeks were going to be trying for him. Turning his world upside down and having to face those who'd undoubtedly denounce him and maybe even threaten his life would take an incredible about of strength. That he was willing to do so in order for her to be his wife — she had no words to describe how special and loved it made her feel or how much she loved him in return. As long as he didn't expect her to give up her dreams — and she knew he wouldn't — she saw no reason to say anything but yes. (300)

Unlike most passing narratives, *Forbidden* ends according to the conventions of the romance genre. With the central obstacle to the lovers' happily ever after resolved, Rhine's public declaration that he has been white passing triggers competing reactions among the people of Virginia City. For the Black population, most of whom speculated on Rhine's racial heritage, there is a sense of relief. For the white population, there is anger. For the most part, that anger is muted, localized in an act of vandalism, the insistence that Rhine resign from the city's council, and the loss of support among members of the town's white Republican party. In a moment of irony, "abolitionist" Lyman Greer angrily demands Rhine hand over the deed to Greer's house. When Rhine asks, "Do you have what you owe me in exchange," Greer refuses to pay and says, in reply to Rhine's "a debt is a debt," "not when it's owed to one of you" (326).

Greer is stunned to discover not only is the debt in full force but owed to Rhine's banker brother, who "counts some of the city's finest lawyers and judges among his clientele" (326). As if that fact wasn't enough, Rhine adds, "And for the record, he's White just like you. I've been kind enough not to ask you for payments. My brother will not be" (326). For the most part, the reaction of the town's white people is limited to an act of vandalism against Rhine's saloon and enraged glares. The Black community, however, comes together for one of their own. Although Zeke's resentment is understood, Rhine is unwilling to engage in a "pissing match" in order to have the damaged windows of his saloon replaced. Unable to fathom Rhine's actions, Zeke asks, "So are you really Colored?" Rhine answers, "I am," and Zeke cannot help but ask, "Why change races now? You had life by the tail. Wealth, respect, and all the privileges that go with it." In a moment guaranteed to send any romance reader into a swoon, Jenkins writes, "Rhine decided he [Zeke] might as well know. 'So I can marry Eddy.' Zeke froze. 'To have her, it was an easy choice'" (337).

What follows for the next two chapters is a familiar scenario in passing narratives where the protagonist's Blackness is "exposed." Rhine's reveal becomes the talk of the town and he is subjected to the racism he'd witnessed directed at other Black citizens. The most telling moment comes when he enters the bank he had patronized since he settled in Virginia City. The young white male clerk informs Rhine "he hadn't the time to give Rhine a list of the transactions that had recently crossed his account" and "suggested Rhine wait until Whitman Brown came to work the next day" (342). His temper already frayed, Rhine insists on seeing the bank's president. The clerk declares, "Mister Peyton doesn't deal with you people." Rhine ignores the clerk and makes his way to Peyton's door. To the clerk's utter humiliation, Peyton merely says, "in a voice that held quiet fury, 'As you already know, Mr. Fontaine is one of this bank's biggest and most loyal depositors. Shall I fire you to prove that point?'" (343). The banker's words make clear that money talks. This is something that Rhine understands quite well.

The critical moment in the novel comes soon after, when a deranged Natalie Greer kidnaps Eddy. When Eddy asks, "Where are we going?," Natalie replies, "To the place where Rhine found you, and this time you're going to die" (351). From the moment Rhine revealed the pass, Natalie has been in denial. She believes he is "lying" and she tells Eddy, "You're the only reason he denounced his race, but he can't marry you if you're dead ... and once you are dead, he'll tell the truth about being White, and he and I can marry the way we were supposed to" (352). Spying the rescue party, Eddy and the driver, who refuses to "take part," take off in a run. Despite her Eddy's prayer that Natalie was ignorant of the weapon she held, both Eddy and the driver are shot. The driver is dead but Eddy is badly wounded. Rhine and Jim commandeer Lyman Greer's buggy and hurry Eddy back to town.

While Rhine waits the outcome of Eddy's surgery, a train conductor enters accompanied by two young Black girls, "their shabby dresses were stained and both girls appeared tired and wan" (355). The conductor asks for Eddy and Rhine recognizes them, "Regan and Portia?" In a heartbreaking scene, we learn the sisters have been "mailed ... by train" to Eddy (355). After asking if the girls want food or to sit, Rhine is shocked by Portia's demand that he "just leave us alone, okay." Not knowing the sisters' background, Rhine recognizes their wariness and asks if they prefer he and Jim stepped outside. When Regan says, "Yes," he and Jim sit out on the back steps (356–57).

Once Eddy regains consciousness, she sees her nieces. After a painful hug, she reassures them she's not dying and asks how they came to be in Virginia City. Portia tells her and says there's a letter from the girls' mother. Assured the girls are staying with her and Sylvie, Eddy asks for Rhine. When the girls back away from the bed, Portia's expression "sour[s]," and Eddy wonders but decides to wait to investigate. As her health improves, Eddy tells Rhine about her nieces' background. After he departs, she discovers why the girls are with her in a letter addressed to her: "It read: I'm getting married. My new husband doesn't want the girls because they aren't his, so they're yours now. It was the coldest, most callous thing Eddy had ever read" (361).

When Regan declares, "Mama doesn't want us, so we don't want her," Eddy recognizes she would be the one to bring her nieces some happiness. She tells the sisters about her relationship with Rhine, and her forthcoming marriage to him. She explains that the sisters will live with her and Rhine. Eddy is surprised, although she shouldn't be, when Portia asks, "how long will he stay with you?" Eddy reassures them her marriage to Rhine is for life and she "will only have relations with him" and it doesn't involve him paying for sex (362). The final question appalls Eddy — "Will we have to have relations with him?" When Eddy learns the reason behind Portia's question, "Mama said she was going to sell Portia's cherry for money," she stares at the sisters, "so angry ... she wanted to walk to Denver and beat her [sister] to death." Instead, Eddy says, "Here you're both safe from anything like that. I promise. Okay? I'm not going to let anyone hurt you, and neither will Rhine" (363).

The novel concludes with the celebration of Rhine and Eddy's marriage once Eddy is fully recovered from her injuries. With his brother Andrew at his side, Rhine and Eddy listen to the sheriff recite the words of matrimony. When the sheriff asks if anyone has issues with the marriage, a female voice offers her objection. "Both Rhine and Eddy turned in shock and a woman walked up. She was as fair-skinned and as green-eyed as Rhine, and beside her was a big dark-skinned man wearing a scowl. Rhine's eyes widened, 'Sable?'" (365). After a joyous reunion, it is Sable's husband Raimond LeVeq who brings real closure to Rhine's complex life when he states, "'I see your bride's a woman of color, Sergeant Clark [Rhine's pseudonym while serving in the US Army]. Hope this means you're back on the right side of the road.' Rhine drops his head and chuckles" (365) before he and Eddy embark on their happily ever after.

Jenkins's representation of white passing is atypical because she refuses to allow her characters to perform the trope of the "tragic mulatto." In *Indigo*, Jenkins has Galen Vachon interrogate the ideologies of race and colorism just as effectively as Rhine. However, unlike Rhine's decision (which is economically driven), Galen treats white passing entirely as a performative act and not as an attempt to avoid his Blackness. He tells the heroine Hester Wyatt that he routinely passes as white in his abolitionist efforts:

> Because of my ancestry, impersonating a French Creole from New Orleans was a fairly easy task. Back then I passed myself off as foreign every time I stepped on American soil. It was my way of ridiculing the Black Code restrictions on travel and accommodations. You'd be surprised how many people are impressed when you claim to be a Brazilian ambassador or a crown prince of Portugal, especially when I can speak the language and they can speak nothing but a backwater drawl. I even posed as an Italian-speaking Haitian count one even to dazzle the registration clerk at one of Baltimore's finest hotels …. People often times see what you want them to see. (Jenkins 1996, 286–87)

Galen's performative act is a necessary part of his political activism to rescue and aid enslaved people seeking freedom. In fact, when he and Hester first meet it is because Galen has been injured when he reveals his "passing" performance. Throughout the novel, Galen uses his skin color, his proximity to whiteness, to undermine not just the actions of the men and women who hunt the escaped enslaved, but he also exposes the fallacy of white supremacy. Elam's observation is worth noting here:

> those who can pass not only inherit the legacies of mixed race heritage; they put that heritage into practice in a way that marks the transgression of, and thus lays bare, the paradox of unequal entitlements in the land of equality. This is why passing creates such cultural anxiety and yet why, too, it holds so much progressive potential. ...by understanding the performance of passing as always politically implicated in the larger possibilities for social change. (Elam 2018, 245)

In other words, both Galen and Rhine shine "a spotlight on not just the constructedness of but also the purposes to which race is put" (245).

As Marcia Alesan Dawkins notes about Frances Harper's *Iola Leroy*,

> access to reality is sometimes based on fiction rather than fact and that identities are understood best in terms of the stories we tell about who we are. Harper reveals how fiction can sometimes ring more "true" than fact and that what we call facts are sometimes simply eloquent and persuasive fictions — fictions we deem most reasonable and expedient" (Dawkins 2012, 79).

Furthermore, Dawkins argues,

> passing ultimately exposes the inability of law to contain racial property in the face of persuasive and powerful rhetorical performances. Passing unmasks our desire to crystallize racial identities as property because they are something we want to possess even though we somehow know we never can. Upholding and obtaining racial property rights becomes a matter of principle in

a world that says some identities are better or worse than others.
(Dawkins 2012, 155)

Like many of the theorists whose work I have cited, I believe white passing
is rife with competing rules of recognition. And, because of the illogic of
white supremacy, these rules are predicated on oppositions tied to a set
of normative standards associated with epidermal, behavioral, or cultural
difference. Moreover, the fact that one group can "recognize" the performance of white passing while another is completely ignorant is what
makes the pass successful. This awareness is always known to the passing
individual, but how does the "in-group," the community capable of recognizing the "performative act," become the "in-group"? In other words, how
do we recognize the "pass" when the passing subject is in middle of the
pass, and how does that passing subject create an informed community
to recognize the pass even when the passing subject needs to remain in
the performative act? In *Forbidden*, Rhine's biological siblings both know
about his white passing and, especially his visibly Black sister, argue for an
end to the performative act.

    What happens, however, when there is no "Black" or familial "in-group"
to keep the white passer's secret? How does the passer, if they wish to
leave evidence of their lineage, their Blackness, ensure traces of history
remain beyond to tell "their story"? The next chapter embraces these
questions as a speculative and heuristic framework for engaging the writings and biographical/autobiographical history of the early modern English author Aphra Behn. As part of complicating, disturbing, muddying the
waters of racial ideologies, white supremacy, and racism, I ask the question, what if Behn was white passing, and explore answers through the
narrative lens of several of her romance novels. Before the Behn acolytes
rise up in arms, let me state that my discussion isn't an attempt to document a Black Aphra. Rather, Behn becomes a template to expose the fallacy of race as colorism. There is some difficulty in what I propose: in
order for a pass to be successful, there has to be a relationship of complicity between the passer and an "in-group," usually a person (or persons)
who has the ability to recognize the signs of performative white passing
and acquiesces to the pass by not exposing it. When the pass is exposed,
either by the passer or a member of the "in-group" or by someone from

the "duped group," it ceases to be a passing performance. Success, therefore, comes when only the duped group remains ignorant.

The presumed "visibility" of whiteness is the source of the passer's ability to convince the "duped group" that what it sees is "true." In effect, passing is acutely dependent upon the idea that what is visible is "an epistemological guarantee" of a historical racial identity. Yet, as the literature of passing indicates, no matter how successful the pass is in public, the passing subject is always burdened by the past they strive to conceal. In literature, this "burden" is often articulated in moments of doubt, internalized fears of discovery (especially when the passing subject is married), and distrust of the very community the passing subject figures as the "in-group." In what follows, I read Aphra Behn's depiction of her life as a performative act of white passing and that her success represents the recognizable signs of that performance.

The thought that floats before me, that has sat with me the many years I have read, pondered, and analyzed the writings of Behn is whether, in the silent space of the poet's room (even when, as may have been the case with Behn, it is a chamber filled with people), the author's own subjectivity came into existence as a memoir of a moment that was a remembrance of a racialized past? Did Behn glance out a small window overlooking a busy street in St Bride's Parish and see a dark-skinned woman of African ancestry struggling to deal with the life of servitude engendered by the color of her skin? Did Behn mentally strip the blouse from the woman's back and see the evidence of the woman's resistance to slavery, to rape? Did Behn imagine the African man who had fathered the woman's first child and died trying to prevent both from becoming property of the Portuguese, Dutch, or English slaver? Did Behn unconsciously perceive in the woman the liminal figure of a daughter whose "mestizaje" (mixedness) drew the sexual attention of a white planter in Barbados? Are these the constitutive images, the "secret ciphers," along with her own passing subjectivity, inscribed in her representation of Moorea or the pregnant Bellamora? Are these the representations of "self" that constitute Behn's "other"?

Chapter Five

Looking and Seeing

In 1668, Aphra Behn was pleading for relief and protection from her indebtedness. Two years later, she would witness the opening and successful six-day run of her first play, *The Forced Marriage* and embark on a career of writing that traversed genres and brought her into the highest circles of the Restoration literati. In her work, Behn did not hesitate to engage the intersectionality of gender, class, and race in both conventional ways (*Abdelazer* and *Oroonoko*) and unconventional ways (*The Widow Ranter*). Most scholarly studies of Behn's canon largely focus on the intersectional threads she weaves together. For example, the majority of critical takes on Behn's romance novels or her dramatic works examine gender issues, especially around women's sexuality or economic concerns. When critics turn to questions of race, the primacy of *Oroonoko* is unquestioned, although *Abdelazer* occasionally gets a nod. Rarely do scholars look to a pair of Behn's novellas as sites to explore questions of race, racism, and colorism — *The Adventure of the Black Lady* (hereafter *The Black Lady*) and *The Unfortunate Bride*, most likely written before her death but not published until 1697. Despite being described as "A Novel," *The Black Lady* hardly seems to reflect what we have come to recognize as a novel; the text is six pages in length and lacks character depth and structural complexity.

Part of the reason these texts may not receive critical attention can be traced to modern editorial decisions that ignore Behn's titles and consign the works to a volume with labels such as *The Black Lady*, *The Fair Jilt*, and *Other Short Stories*. The other, and more significant reason, is the debate on early modern prose fiction and whether it can be called a "novel" or not. For example, Michael McKeon writes, "seventeenth- and early eighteenth-century writers often use the terms 'romance,' 'history,' and 'novel' with an evident interchangeability that must bewilder and frustrate all modern expectations" (McKeon 1987, 25). Moreover, McKeon continues, "alongside this confusion we can perceive a growing impulse to make the dyad 'romance/history' stand for an all-but-absolute dichotomy between opposed ways of knowing the world" (25). As a result, romance is posited "not only as a distinct generic, but also as broadly epistemological, category whose meaning is overwhelmingly trivializing or pejorative" (27). Yet, as McKeon contends, "the casual pretense to historical truth … is one of the traditional romance methods of self-authentication" (56). Ironically, McKeon reminds us, "the claim to historicity is no less a rhetorical trope than verisimilitude" (53). It is, in the end, the "dyad 'romance/history'" that allowed for the hybrid that is the late seventeenth-century novel.

The novel, according to Lennard J. Davis, has its basis in history, has a more contemporary locale (usually that of the author), and is "shorter and more compact of plot," while "romances value the preservation of virtue and chastity; novels tend to focus on illegal doings and forbidden passions" (Davis 1996, 40). Furthermore, Davis argues, "romances make clear that they are mixing fact and fiction to create an essentially fictional plot; novels tend to deny that they are fictional" (40). Leah Orr rightly criticizes the efforts of critics such as McKeon, Davis, and others to develop "theories about the differences between romances and novels, between fact and fiction, between Behn and Defoe. They have mostly sought development, progress, and evolution in the texts of canonical authors" (Orr 2017, 26). As she points out,

> the language used to describe works of fiction and the comments made about factual and fictional writing in the eighteenth century is far more complex and nuanced than most modern critics have acknowledged. Writers of fiction were conscious of what they were doing, and what their readers might want, and to base our ideas about early fiction on the work of just a few authors seriously misrepresents the wide range of fiction available in the period (27).

Janet Todd's decision to classify what Behn refers to as novels as "short stories" performs two actions. (Todd 1997) First, it ignores the complexities of the romance novel structure, which is not always determined by form, and plays into modern expectations about the novel form. And, by referring to the novellas as "short stories," Todd makes these texts more easily dismissible when it comes to considerations of Behn's self-representation and the questions of race and racism. Second, and this is a fundamental flaw in critical approaches to Behn's engagement with race, the erasure of these texts as "romance novels" misses the generic work that they do and plays into a reification of *Oroonoko* as Behn's "real" romance novel. In what follows, I want to step away from the theoretical arguments about what constitutes the distinction between romance and novel. I read both *The Black Lady* and *The Unfortunate Bride* as Behn designated them, novels, with an understanding that these two texts participate in a literary economy of racializing subjectivity but not necessarily in the way critical studies of Behn's canon seems to take for granted. It is my argument that the deceptive simplicity of *The Unfortunate Bride* and *The Black Lady*, when the pair are read in tandem, offers a complex picture of Behn crafting a strategic relationship to white supremacist logic about Blackness and whiteness as stable somatic signs.

The Unfortunate Bride

The Unfortunate Bride presents a familiar Behn romance storyline. The novel begins with two male friends, Frankwit and Wildvill, "both with considerable fortunes although "Wildvill was of the richest family, but Frankwit of the noblest" (Behn 1915, 377). After some time praising Frankwit's qualities, the narrator tells the reader "Belvira only boasted Charms to move him ... and from their childhood they felt mutual love." Like most of Behn's romances, parental intervention separates the loves when, in Belvira's "fourteenth year," her father sends her to London not long after her mother's death. Apparently, Frankwit's father also "took a journey to the other world," and with "all imaginable haste" Frankwit buried his father and rushed off to London (378). Eighteen months pass with many solicitations on Frankwit's part and refusal to consummate their love on Belvira's part.

The exchange between the lovers ends with Belvira agreeing to wed Frankwit based on his promise of fidelity, "my dear Belvira ... be assured I shall be ever yours, as you are mine; fear not you shall never draw Bills of Love upon me so fast, as I shall wait in readiness to pay them" (382). Immediately upon mentioning "Bills," Frank informs Belvira he is off to Cambridgeshire and will return within a week with a "Brace of thousand pounds" to celebrate their nuptials. The lovers exchange letters written in verse, which Belvira shares with her formerly blind cousin, Celesia. According to Belvira's last letter, "an aged matron has by charms unknown" cured Celesia's blindness. Frankwit's pleasure in this letter, and the others from Belvira, proves to be his downfall, "for 'twas that very fondness proved his ruin" as he "often read the letters o're and o're" (385). At this point in the novel, we might expect a father's or relative's intervention or a lover's sudden bankruptcy as the obstacle to love. What Behn offers, and what we do not see in any of her other romances, is disruptive sexuality in the form of a Black woman.

While in Cambridgeshire, Frankwit took lodgings

> at a cousin's house of his, and there, (it being a private family) lodged likewise a Blackamoor Lady, then a Widower; a whimsical Knight had taken a fancy to enjoy her: Enjoy her did I say? Enjoy the Devil in the Flesh at once! I know not how it was, but he would fain have been a Bed with her, but she not consenting on unlawful terms, (but sure all Terms are with her unlawful) the Knight soon marry'd her, as if there not hell enough in matrimony, but he must wed the Devil too. The knight a little after died, and left this Lady of his (whom I shall call Moorea) an estate of six thousand pounds per Ann. (541)

Behn's characterization of Moorea is marked by a series of surprising turns we don't often see in early modern literary depictions of Black women. For all the pejorative, religiously-inflected anti-Black rhetoric, Behn doesn't leave those as our only images of Moorea. She is a Lady, widow, and possesses "an estate of six thousand pounds per Ann." In other words, the Lady Moorea is nobility by virtue of her marriage.

Behn's representation of Moorea, even with the negative language we often see linked to Black characters (evil, lust driven, duplicitous, jealous, and so on), is of an independent woman who can afford to act on her desires. Moorea does not articulate a worry about how she will economically survive. She doesn't need to seek a husband for her erotic pleasures. Most importantly, Moorea is a Lady. Despite the narrator's racist approbation about how the marriage came to be, Moorea clearly recognizes the problems attendant on unmarried sexuality. On this point, I find Jacqueline Pearson's point that Behn's "romantic affirmations ... are constantly undercut by financial realities, for the tales are anchored in economic as much as erotic desire" (Pearson 2004, 195). Therefore, I would argue, the only real difference between the women in the romance comes down to who controls her financial destiny, and the answer is Moorea.

Once Frankwit's betrayal of his betrothed is known, Belvira considers him lost to her and eventually marries Wildvill. Of course, the romance plot requires closure for at least one of the rivals. Frankwit, "tho, yet extremely weak," rides to London and arrives on the day of the marriage. At this point Behn deploys one of her favorite strategies for authenticity of the account, deploying the authorial "I." Behn uses this technique in a number of her romances, the most notable use occurs in *Oroonoko*. In *The Unfortunate Bride*, the author states,

> I was at this time in Cambridge, and having some small acquaintance with this Blackmoor Lady, and sitting in her Room that evening, after Frankwit's departure thence, in Moorea's absence, saw inadvertently a bundle of Papers, which she had gathered up, as I suppose, to burn, since now they grew but useless, she having no farther Hopes of him: I fancy'd I knew the Hand, and thence my Curiosity only led me to see the Name and finding Belvira subscrib'd, I began to guess there was some foul play in Hand. Belvira being my particularly intimate Acquaintance, I read one of them, and finding the Contents, convey'd them all secretly out with me, as I thought, in Point of Justice I was bound, and sent them to Belvira by that Night's Post; so that they came to her Hands soon after the Minute of her Marriage, with an Account how, and by what Means I came to light on them. (473)

The remainder of *The Unfortunate Bride* details in typical romance-genre fashion the discovery of the truth behind Frankwit's betrayal/abandonment, the duel between Frankwit and Wildvill (who believes Belvira is Frankwit's "Strumpet"), the revelation of the misunderstanding (all laid at Moorea's feet) of the deaths of Wildvill and Belvira, and Belvira's insistence that Frankwit marry her formerly-blind cousin. Thus, while Frankwit and

Belvira didn't achieve their happily ever after, Celesia and Frankwit do. Moorea, the presumed instigator, appears to escape punishment for acting on her desires.

The one detail that casts Behn's depiction of Moorea in an interesting light is when the author intrudes to comment that she was "in Cambridge" and had "some small acquaintance with this Blackmoor Lady" (473). As Pearson rightly argues, these types of intrusions serve as the "author-narrator's desire to insist on the truth of the narrative and the eye-witness authority of the narrator" (Pearson 2004, 195). I want to suggest that the detail should invite more scrutiny. Until this moment, we have very little information about the authorial voice. The romance begins with an account of the friendship between Frankwit and Wildvill. Most the narrative is in the third person except for the moment the narrator "secretly" conveys the letters from Moorea's room (Moorea being absent) and sends them to Belvira who was a "particularly intimate Acquaintance" of the narrator. What is significant is that once the author-narrator sends the letters to Belvira, both Moorea and the authorial "I" disappear from the romance plot. On the surface, the use of the authorial "I" as eye-witness may seem trivial. However, we see this convention pop up enough times in Behn's romance novels (e.g., *Oroonoko*) to recognize that it has an additional purpose.

The Black Lady

We see this technique used in *The Black Lady*. It opens as follows, "about the Beginning of Last June (as near as I can remember) Bellamora came to town from Hampshire" (Behn 1915, 7). The intrusive "I" services to establish the veracity of the narrative. The precision of the narrative details creates a historical authenticity (London) that underscores the romance elements despite the idealized names. The end result, not surprisingly, is the continued instability of ontological and thus historical certainty. Even so, Behn's novel does align itself more with romance than history: the idealized names (Mrs. Brightly, Bellamora, Fondlove, and so on); the vagueness of Bellamora's history; and the allegorical ending to the novel.

Seduced by her lover and pregnant with his child, Bellamora leaves her home in Hampshire and travels to London, in search of "Madam Brightly, a

Relation of hers with whom she design'd to continue for about a half a year undiscover'd, if possibly, by her Friends in the Country" (315). Upon her arrival at London, Bellamora loses her "Trunk, with her Clothes, and most of her Money and Jewels." She is taken up by an "ancient Gentlewoman," who after hearing Bellamora's pitiful tale, recognizes the lover's name and brings Bellamora's situation to the attention of a gentlewoman residing in the house. The woman happens to be the sister of Fondlove (for so the lover is named). The two women (landlady and Fondlove's sister) contrive to bring the two lovers together by persuading Bellamora that, if she does not wed Fondlove, she will be sent to the "House of Correction, and her Child to a Parish-Nurse" (319). Bellamora refuses all attempts to prod her into marriage until a desperate Fondlove invokes the one argument against which (it is supposed) no woman's tenacity can prevail — maternal instinct:

> But he taking her in his Arms began again, as he was wont to do, with Tears in his Eyes, to beg that she wou'd marry him e'er she was delivered; if not for his, nor her own, yet for the Child's sake, which she hourly expected; that it might not be born out of Wedlock, and so be made uncapable of inheriting either of their Estates, with a great many more pressing Arguments on all sides. (320)

Bellamora's resistance is finally broken and at last she consents.

Of the numerous novelistic writings Behn produced, it is intriguing that *The Black Lady* has received very little scholarly attention. In *The Secret Life of Aphra Behn*, Todd suggestively implies that Behn may not have written *The Black Lady* (Todd 1997). According to Todd, the likely candidate is Tom Brown, who satirized Behn in his *Letters to the Dead from the Living* and who translated Scarron into English for Samuel Briscoe (publisher, along with Charles Gildon, of *The Histories and Novels of the Late Ingenious Mrs. Behn* 1696). Todd's explanation for the possible ascription to Brown is that, when Behn's "The King of Bantam" was published in 1698 (in a second edition of *The Histories and Novels*), Gildon worried about the difference between Behn's baroque prose fiction style and that of the new work: "The Stile of the Court of the King of Bantam, being so very different from Mrs. Behn's usual way of Writing, it may perhaps call its being genuine into Question." The answer he gives is that it was done for a wager to see if she could write in Scarron's style. (Todd 1997, 317)

The Black Lady appeared for the first time in the 1698 All the Histories and Novels of Mrs. Aphra Behn. In her discussion of Behn's novel, Todd writes:

> Like "The Court of the King of Bantam," "The Black Lady" dates itself by reference to a theatrical performance: of John Wilson's The Cheats. It too has self-conscious touches of Behn. Having lost trunk and friends in alien London, the dark-haired heroine responds by sending out for a "Pint of Sack." But other curious elements are less typical. Proving pregnant, the heroine keeps her room to hide her "great Belly." One of the Scarron stories that [Tom] Brown translated was "The Useless Precaution," in which the man's beloved kept her room because she was in the last stages of pregnancy. In her condition, the "Black Lady" is forced by her officious friends to choose life on the parish or marriage to a man she has come to loathe; the overseers of the poor who search for her are called rapacious "wolves" who prey on the poor. Is this Behn getting at her father? Or Brown, knowing more than most, getting at Behn? (Todd 1997, 317)

Todd's comments merit some consideration. First, it is clear that she is not entirely convinced that Behn wrote The Black Lady. The only "touches of Behn" Todd identifies is that Bellamora sends "out for a 'Pint of Sack.'" What, we might ask, about the novel's opening sentence? The character names? The playful pun that concludes the novel? More importantly, the narrative refusal to lay blame (a rather common feature in Behn's complex handling of gender relations within her writings)?

Todd's suggestive questions about the possible motive behind the writing of The Black Lady similarly require more than she offers. Why would Behn write a story of a pregnant woman to get "at her father" (especially when, by Todd's own account, Behn's father died enroute to Surinam nearly 30 years before), or Brown, "knowing more than most," want to get "at Behn"? In some ways, Todd's comments would have been far more convincing had she merely stated the fact that *The Black Lady* was published in *All the Histories and Novels of Mrs. Aphra Behn* and end her discussion of the text there. Or, if Todd wanted to engage critically the novel and its intriguing history, addressing questions of ascription, style, and interpretation, her discussion of *The Black Lady* should have been more than a single paragraph. In all fairness to Todd, it must be acknowledged that her principal aim in writing *The Secret Life of Aphra Behn* is biographical and not literary analysis. Yet the tantalizing questions Todd poses about authorial motive for writing *The Black Lady* (whether the author is Behn or Brown) deserve further analysis and/or commentary. Interestingly, Todd ignores completely Behn's provocative title and its implication.

Pearson, on the other hand, not only accepts Behn's authorship of *The Black Lady* but also takes up the matter of the novel's title. In her essay "Slave Princes and Lady Monsters: Gender and Ethnic Difference in the Work of Aphra Behn," Pearson considers the novel in light of Behn's general use of "images of racial and cultural difference" throughout her work (Pearson 1996). Pearson's analysis explores Behn's use of racial and monstrous images in a number of texts — *Oroonoko*, *The Unfortunate Bride*, *Abdelazer*, and *The Rover*. When Pearson turns her attention to *The Black Lady*, she observes, "the protagonist Bellamore is, presumably, only 'black' in the usual seventeenth-century meaning of the word, dark-haired and dark-eyed. But her name, while representing 'bell'amora,' 'beautiful love,' can also be read as 'bella mora,' 'beautiful Moor.' Pregnant, unprotected, unmarried and consequently persecuted in Restoration society, she is thus identified by implication with the position of Blacks as outsiders" (Pearson 1996, 226). Unlike Todd, Pearson astutely highlights one of the intriguing lexical complexities associated with Behn's practice of naming her fictional characters. Behn's audience presumably would have easily recognized the playful semantics denoted by Bellamora's name.

Despite drawing attention to the novel's title, *The Adventure of the Black Lady*, and the multiple semantics of Bellamora's name, Pearson does not expand on either point. Furthermore, with reference to the novel's title, Pearson's comment that "Bellamora is, presumably, only 'black' in the usual seventeenth-century meaning of the word, dark-haired and dark-eyed" is a somewhat paradoxical and misleading statement. Pearson's comment first implies that there is only one presumable way to read Behn's use of "black," "dark-haired and dark-eyed," yet later suggests that (given Bellamora's name) we should comprehend her identification "by implication with the position of Blacks as outsiders." The word "black," as Pearson suggests, was used routinely to describe an individual with dark hair and eyes. However, and this is a significant caveat, the word also signified skin color (Black Moor, Black woman, and so on) and the hair and eye color of most dark-skinned people was also dark. This semantic register does not in and of itself negate Pearson's definition; rather, it expands and complicates the interpretive range of the novel's ideological meaning (as Pearson's observation suggestively implies). Furthermore, if we were to read The Black Lady as a romance (as I believe we should), then Pearson's final point, linking Bellamora's identity "with the position of Blacks as outsiders," has far greater ideological significance than both she and Todd acknowledge.

With the exception of Pearson, few scholars draw attention to the idea of reading The Black Lady in terms of race. Two arguments sum up what would be general opposition to this idea: first, the novel's title and Bellamora's name notwithstanding, nowhere in the novel does Behn specifically describe or refer to Bellamora in terms of racial (that is, Black) attributes; and second, if Behn had wanted Bellamora to be viewed as "Black" she would have done so since Behn rarely displayed reluctance to represent Blacks in her other writings (Oroonoko, Abdelazer, or Moorea, the "Blackamoor Lady," in The Unfortunate Bride). This opposition is valid if certain principles exist trans-historically as definitive truths — that the semantics and semiotics of race are always monochrome; that white passing did not exist prior to the late nineteenth century as a cultural phenomenon of the transatlantic slave trade; and that every literary treatment with race will always assume the same form — anti-Blackness.

I make this point because the analysis of race in Renaissance and early modern English culture often operates according to these principles. Yet, as the literary tradition of color passing demonstrates, the certainty by which human beings recognize and know racial identification is easily undone. One of the complexities in thinking about race and white passing in early modern English literary texts is the question of evidence. We are accustomed, at least in the United States, to viewing racial passing as particular to enslavement and the rise of very specific white-centric notions about how racial differences are discerned and, in literature, displayed. What Heliodorus's *Aethiopika* has shown is that reading for the somatic isn't always reliable. I propose that *The Black Lady* exemplifies this same "truth" when it comes to racial recognition. In other words, it is my contention that the author insists that we disentangle ourselves from normative expectations about evidentiary predicates of race.

The heroine of Behn's romance, Bellamora, possesses all the ideal attributes that a late seventeenth-century romance heroine should: "Youth, Beauty, Education, Family and Estate" (319). The narrator's use of phrases such as "Fair Innocent (I must not say Foolish) one," "The Fair Unthinking Creature," or "the pretty innocent Creature," suggests that, for all her "Education," Bellamora is extremely naïve (316). Yet there are moments in the narrative where we must wonder whether she is as "innocent" as portrayed. For example, it is not entirely certain that Bellamora has conveyed the truth of her experiences to the Land-Lady:

> the discreet Gentlewoman endeavour'd to comfort her [Bellamora] by all the softest and most powerful Argument in her Capacity ... which she did with so much Earnestness and visible Integrity, that the pretty innocent Creature was going to make her a full and real Discovery of her imaginary, insupportable Misfortunes; and (doubtless) had done it; had she not been prevented by the Return of the Lady, whom she hop'd to have found her Cousin Brightly. (316)

Bellamora's reticence in revealing her real situation is both an astute move when one travels to a new environment yet, the next morning, she reveals all to the "Land-Lady" and another "Lady" who we soon discover is the sister of Fondlove. Bellamora's description of her relationship with Fondlove is a curious account. Throughout her account, her disinterest in Fondlove is apparent; her uncle's attempt to wed her to a man "whose Person and Humour did by no means hit with my Inclinations" (317). "This," she continues, "gave Fondlove the unhappy Advantage over me." What then transpires is a classic example of seduction. However, instead of the lover repudiating the beloved, it is the pregnant Bellamora who is reluctant, declaring "'Tis the only thing I dread in this World: For I am certain he can never love me after: Besides, ever since, I have abhorr'd the Sigh of him" (38). Only when faced with the threat of imprisonment and the loss of her child does Bellamora finally agree to wed her seducer (Behn makes it difficult to view Fondlove as Bellamora's lover); even so it is with great reluctance:

> He taking her in his Arms began again, as he was wont to do, with Tears in his Eyes, to beg that she wou'd marry him e'er she was delivered; if not for his, nor her own, yet for the Child's sake, which she hourly expected; that it might not be born out of Wedlock, and so be made uncapable of inheriting either of their Estates; with a great many more pressing Arguments on all sides: To which at last she consented. (320)

Unlike Behn's other novellas and novels, love seems not to be as great a factor in this storyline as one might expect.

The Black Lady ends on what can only be viewed as a rather bizarre note:

> Whilst they [Bellamora and Fondlove] were abroad, came the Vermin of the Parish, (I mean, the Overseers of the poor, who eat the Bread from 'em) to search for a young Black-hair'd Lady (for so was Bellamora) who was either brought to bed, or just ready to lie down. The Land-Lady shew'd 'em all the Rooms of her House, but no such Lady cou'd be found. At last she bethought her self, and led 'em into her Parlour, where she open'd a little Closet-door, and shew'd 'em her Black Cat that had just kitten'd assuring 'em, that she shou'd never trouble the Parish as long as she had Rats or Mice in the House, and so dismiss'd 'em like Logger-heads as they came. (320)

The Land-Lady's feline humor serves to bring closure to Bellamora's troubles in true romantic fashion. Bellamora and Fondlove are reunited and married and all possible threats to their relationship/happiness effectively thwarted. Yet there is the fact that the humor in the text's final words is premised on the metaphoric association between Bellamora and the cat in terms of their "similar" color.

What are we to make of this romance novel and its wordplay? On the one hand, *The Black Lady* stands as little more than an exercise in romance storytelling. Behn's text is terse to an extreme, dependent on stereotypes, and simplistic in its plotting. When compared to Behn's other novels, the romance seems to fall well short of the novelistic mark in terms of how deeply Behn engages her usual themes. What Behn does, when we consider the text as an example of an ideological register fraught with racial complexity, cannot be easily ignored. Both the novel's title and the name of its female protagonist invite us to speculate on Behn's purpose in framing her story in what clearly would be recognized (even in the seventeenth century) as racializing predicates. Bellamora, despite the dual signification of her name, is marked racially by the novel's title and her own name. The "whiteness" of Bellamora, therefore, is a priori questioned, if not thoroughly destabilized, as a signifier of the ordering of female beauty along a color spectrum. The idealization of whiteness, and the continuing degradation of Blackness, contributed greatly to the use of the word "race" as a predicate of color by the time Behn embarked on her writing career.

In addition, the word "Moor" was always a racialized term of color in pre- and early modern English culture and language as witnessed by the delineation of Moors according to color ("Blackamoor," "Tawny Moor," white "Moor") that surfaced occasionally in texts. Language begets imagery, and imagery begets meaning, and Bellamora's "fairness" sits in obvious juxtaposition to this African-ness. Hence, Behn offers a playful reminder that, when translating the word Bellamora, we cannot never foreclose meaning — Bellamora will always translate into English as both "the beautiful Moor" and "beautiful love." Thus, Bellamora's fairness exists always in contrast to her name, neither allowing the novel's readers to ignore the relationship between naming and seeing, nor fostering a privileged hierarchy of beauty. *The Black Lady* is clearly inscribed on such terrain despite its length; and, in my view, this terrain prescribes how we are to read the text.

From the title to the novel's culminating jest, Blackness that is "fair" (i.e., white) constitutes the racialized identity that is Bellamora. This effect is achieved in large measure through Behn's adroit use of romance's de-familiarizing techniques — verisimilitude and allegory, history and the fantastic. The romance tradition allows Behn to destabilize readerly expectations about the absolute knowability of a person's racial identity based on color. In this, *The Black Lady* continues the tradition constituted in representations such as Heliodorus's Charikliea and Franklin/Tasso's Clorinda. What all three female characters make clear is that the social category of "Black" women must be rethought to take account of the white-passing figure. Unlike Charikliea and Clorinda, however, Bellam-ora's racial identity remains a narrative enigma; her mother and father conveniently dead, her uncle unnamed, Bellamora's genealogy is known to us only through her name. In addition, Bellamora's extreme reluctance to wed the man who impregnates her is curiously inexplicable, particularly in a society and age that do not condone pregnancies sans marriage. Her reasons are never made clear, and in the end, only the coercive force of England's legal system seems to tip the scales for Bellamora. The novel's conclusion, even so, remains decidedly unsatisfactory.

If, as I am suggesting, we are being asked to read *The Black Lady* as a passing narrative, we may be witnessing one more version of the Charik-liea/Clorinda narrative, within a more complicated frame of reference. Miscegenation was very much a part of English colonial and metropolitan social and cultural practices in the seventeenth century. The stakes for English/African women similar to Charikliea and Clorinda would be far different in this context. Racial identification increasingly became deter-mined not only along national lines but also along a color spectrum. The privileging of whiteness was concurrent with the absolute denigra-tion of Blackness. While this hierarchizing of color was not new — with the transatlantic slave trade and an increasing redefinition of how one's racial lineage was determined — the visibility or invisibility of Blackness achieved an ontological stature within cultural discourse. And, the choice to be "Black" or "white" not surprisingly assumed an ideological impor-tance among those whose "Blackness" was not visible. In this world, the Bellamoras faced a difficult decision: to declare their "Blackness" and be de-humanized as a "negro," or to use their whiteness and live life as a passing subject.

Assuming Bellamora was one of these women, she must leave behind all that would announce to the world that her "race" and color were not one. She must vigilantly guard against those traces of her past that might expose her deed. She must invent a new narrative, a "plausible history," to ensure her secret: dead parents, an unsympathetic, and perhaps, cruel guardian, a missing relative. Most important, if at all possible, she must avoid marriage. To comprehend Bellamora as a figurative white-passing subject is to understand the unstated in the situations of Charikliea and Clorinda; and, concomitantly, to read Bellamora as actively engaged in color passing is to recognize that the social, political, ideological, and cultural conditions extant in late seventeenth-century England were conducive to such a phenomenon. Finally, to read *The Black Lady* as a white-passing narrative is to explore whether Behn's fictive characterization not only narratively functions to make visible the invisible Blackness that marked all retellings of Heliodorus's romance but also serves as a potentially self-reflective mirroring of the author's complex relationship to late seventeenth-century English white supremacist thinking.

Chapter Six

"Fictions of the Pose": Act I, Scene 2

> Racial identity is always in process and constantly re-created around the dialectical poles of racial essence and/or appearance and racial performance.
>
> (Cutter 2018, 60)

If you have reached this point, dear readers, you will notice *Race and Romance: Coloring the Past* is an unconventional intellectual meandering. Two of early modern English literature's favorite tropes are the window and the mirror, objects of inspection, reflection, and potential deception — each piece of "glass" in its own way assumed to be an accurate or a "true" image of what is being reflected because the window or the mirror absorbs and/or projects what touches its surface. Yet, as early modern English writers often lamented, what was reflected or mirrored could also be a deception. Such is the case in Beverly Jenkins's *Forbidden*. Rhine is dressed for an evening out and Eddy observes him and his reflection in a mirror: "The tailored black suit, the snow white shirt, jet black hair, and vivid eyes all added up to a man as alluring as a god" (Jenkins 2016, 82). The vision the reader "sees" is mediated through Eddy's eyes, she provides the eye-witness account. Rhine says one word to her, "Presentable?" When Eddy replies, "Your tie's a mite crooked," he walks "to the large standing mirror. Upon seeing nothing wrong with the tie, he glances back at her in confusion." Eddy says, "just pulling your leg. You look fine" (82). This brief exchange takes place in that most intimate of spaces, the bedroom — specifically, Rhine's bedroom. This scene intrigues me for it is one of three mentions of a mirror and the only one where our heroine and hero are both present. What Eddy "sees" is a white man, "alluring as a god" and forbidden to her, a romantic impossibility not just because of class but because of his color.

All of the romance texts I have discussed exemplify that appearances are complicated and always performative. The ability to reflect back what is in front of it is the singular purpose of the mirror. What Eddy sees is not what Rhine (and by implication the novel's reader) sees — his Blackness. Similarly, when *Godfrey of Bulloigne*'s Clorinda replaces her "silver" armor with black armor she clouds the viewer's ability to penetrate the veneer of whiteness that obscures her Blackness. *The Isle of Pines* serves as an acknowledgement that whiteness is not only porous but performative. No matter how they are denigrated, the Phils are whiteness walking and, as the novel makes clear, for white supremacy to sustain itself, it is not enough to regulate visibly Black bodies; whiteness itself must be policed. It is important to note that two of the romance authors analyzed in this book are women. Over three hundred years, and the evolution of modern racial capitalism, separate the publications of Aphra Behn's romance novels and those of Beverly Jenkins. Yet, what both authors expose are the cracks and fractures of a society governed by racist and sexist ideologies.

In the form of a "brief treatise," I want to suggest that Behn, caught between competing models of racial performances, was ideally situated to negotiate textually the theater of whiteness. White supremacist anxiety about the purity of whiteness is not localized to the nineteenth and twentieth centuries. On the contrary, as Kim F. Hall brilliantly demonstrates, quoting Patricia Williams, in *Things of Darkness: Economies of Race and Gender in Renaissance England*, "'extrinsic sources and intuitive means of reading may be the only ways to include the reality of the unwritten, unnamed, nontext of race' (117)" (Hall 1995, 15). In effect, it is important to engage in

> a practice of resistant reading that seems key to an enterprise of this sort. To claim that there is a "text of race" means at times to refuse to accept both the authority of the writers I work with and to resist the hegemony of white male knowledge in the academy. I use "intuitive means of reading" in the sense that my reading of dominant culture is fundamentally shaped by knowledge that is in fact taught in African-American communities about "white" culture. I also draw from "extrinsic sources" when I suggest alternative readings and viewpoints regarding the subjects of colonial rule that are largely absent in the period. (Hall 1995, 15)

My argument throughout this book follows this mode of analysis. It is an argument based on an "intuitive reading" that anxiety about the potential for "white passing" sits at the heart of white supremacy. Blackness and whiteness as racial categories are intrinsically unstable should be a foregone conclusion and, yet, the ideology of race insists that they are. One of the central premises of white supremacy is its sense of privilege and superiority in that whiteness. However, as Toni Morrison suggests, behind that notion of "superiority" is "[a] companion to this whiteness — a dark and abiding presence that moves the hearts and texts of ... literature with fear and longing" (Morrison 1992, 80).

What I have suggestively been arguing in this book is that is the source of "fear and longing" is the "white-passing subject." And, unless the Blackness hidden by a white-presenting shell is exposed and the body policed, whiteness' invisibility in the face of Blackness when that Blackness is performing whiteness will always be paradoxical. Because, to return to our mirror and window tropes, the passing performance is visible for all to see yet not all will comprehend its significance.

At the conclusion of their thought-provoking essay on Aphra Behn's *Oroonoko*, Rob Baum writes "[Behn] pauses a moment to contemplate the shape of her world from the insulation of her female body, with its own black secrets" (Baum 2011, 26). The dancing around the edges of Behn's relationship to race and racial identities have marked Behn studies for decades. Most often her racial identity is read through the lens of Oroonoko's Blackness. What if, in addition to *Oroonoko*, we also read her "white-presenting body" as reflectively mirrored in *The Black Lady* and *The Unfortunate Bride*? Simply stated, what if we peel away the layers of performative whiteness to "see" Behn's "Black body"? A body not mirrored in Oroonoko's but in Bellamora's and Moorea's. To do this is to question, to interrogate, the extrinsic valorization of colorism as a means of reading racecraft.

A "Briefe Treatise" on the Making of Aphra Behn

The literary construction of Aphra Behn is fascinating and, dear reader, I apologize in advance for the meandering I am about to undertake. But

making a case for "seeing" Behn as a white-passing subject is best con-
sumed in two parts.

Part I

In 1696, seven years after Aphra Behn's death, the first biographic sketch,
The Memoirs of Mrs. Aphra Behn, Written by a Lady of Quality (hereafter
The Memoirs), was appended to her posthumously-published play *The
Younger Brother*. Since this initial biographical effort to render an account
of Behn's life and literary reputation, the pre-professional life of Aphra
Behn has been revisited, rewritten, expanded, and historically "set in
stone" in an attempt to get at the "truth" of Behn's birth and life: in 1928
by Vita Sackville-West; 1948 by George Woodcock; 1968 by Frederick M.
Link; 1977 by Maureen Duffy; 1980 by Angeline Goreau; and 1997 by Janet
Todd. Reading any and all of the six biographies, it is readily apparent that
the greatest obstacle facing the intrepid scholar interested in Behn's early
life is the absolute paucity of evidence available to abet such an endeavor.
In fact, when we subject to careful scrutiny what is available, the situation
becomes even more indeterminate despite the certainty with which biographers make use of extant materials to substantiate the reported "facts"
of Behn's birth.

The "truths" of Behn's early life (the place of her birth, her father's
appointment, her experiences in Surinam) have been gleaned from a
mélange of fictive enunciation located in a number of texts written either
by Behn, particularly the novella *Oroonoko*, or within the first decade
after her death in 1689 (the Countess of Winchelsea's poem, Thomas
Culpeper's biographic sketch in his *Adversaria*, the brief account attached
to the posthumous publication of one of Behn's plays, and *The Memoirs*).
What remains as holographic evidence, letters to the king's secretary of
state, notes to Jacob Tonson, one of her publishers, and a Pindaric on
the poet Edmund Waller, were all written post-1665. While these documents provide extraordinary insight into Behn's life as an unattached
woman striving to live independently in a society that did not recognize
such independence, they offer limited aid in deciphering the pre-Restora-
tion (or even pre-England) period of her life. Thus, when we compare the
evidence for Behn's life with that of Margaret Cavendish, for example, it

becomes obvious that the project of authenticating, or "reconstructing," a complete life history for the individual named Aphra Behn is daunting to say the least. Even so, there have been six attempts to date.

Since the latter half of the nineteenth century, there have been two possible candidates for the "real" early Aphra Behn: Aphra Amis and Aphra Johnson. Both Aphras were born in Kent in the year 1640. In "An ACCOUNT of the Life of the Incomparable Mrs. BEHN," we find one of the earliest allusions to Behn's patrilineal name: "Her Maiden Name was Johnson" (Duffy 1977, 17). This perception remained unquestioned until the nineteenth century when Edmund Gosse discovered a marginal notation in a manuscript of Anne Finch poems. Presumed to be Finch's own handwriting, the marginalia stated that Behn "was daughter to a barber, who liv'd formerly in Wye, a little market town (now much decay'd) in Kent. Though the account of her life before her works pretends otherwise; some persons now alive do testify upon their knowledge that to be her original." Gosse's investigation led him to conclude that Behn was "the daughter of a barber named John Johnson, [and that] she was baptized at Wye, Kent, 10 July 1640" (Duffy 1977, 19).

Finch's marginal notation appeared to resolve one of the pieces of the puzzle. A search of the birth records for the area surrounding Wye quickly yielded fruit; an Aphra Amis had been born near Wye in 1640, thus corroborating Finch's declaration. Some years later, the Reverend A. Purvis checked the complete records, including burial registers, in Wye and discovered a fact that Gosse had overlooked: the child born in or near Wye, Aphra Amis, had died July 12, 1640. Purvis's finding, not surprisingly, reopened the investigation of Behn's origins. Not until Duffy embarked upon her biography of Behn was the Aphra Amis ascription put to rest. In words that have become increasingly familiar to Behn scholars, Duffy writes:

> The fictions begin with her birth. The account which you will find
> in most works of reference, which is that she was born Aphra Amis
> in the town of Wye in July 1640, is quite untrue. As the present
> vicar very kindly pointed out to me when I wrote to him and as
> had already been noticed, that Aphra died a few days after she
> was born. The whole Aphra Amis legend rested on a note by Anne
> Finch, Countess of Winchelsea, to one of her own poems where

she described Apollo lamenting for Aphra Behn's death .... "From
the banks of the Stoure the desolate Wye, / He lamented for Behn,
o'er that place of her birth". (Duffy 1977, 16)

Duffy's explorations of the birth and burial records produced not only
Finch's Aphra Amis but a second Aphra Amis, the mother of Finch's Aphra.
Duffy also found an Aphra Beane who, she concluded, must have been the
person Finch's native informants had in mind.

Duffy's work led her back to Aphra Johnson. She soon found an Eaffry
(Aphra) Johnson — the daughter of Bartholomew Johnson and Elizabeth
Denham — born in the village of Harbledown near Canterbury in 1640.
The substantive link between Aphra Behn and "Eaffry" Johnson for Duffy
proved to be Thomas Culpeper. In his odd compilation of fact and fiction
called the *Adversaria*, Culpeper writes, "Mrs Aphara Bhen was born at
Canterbury or Sturry, her mother being the Colonell's nurse" (Duffy 1977,
16). The entry goes on to state that he had visited her grave "in the cloister
at Westminster near the door that goes into the church," prompting Duffy
to speculate that "perhaps he was even at her funeral." Taking Culpeper at
his word, Duffy notes that "the Colonell" is Thomas Culpeper himself and
concludes that "in default of a better candidate Eaffry Johnson seems to
fulfill most of the requirements, including Thomas Culpepper's statement
that she was born in Sturry or Canterbury. Harbledown virtually is Canterbury. The Sturry registers record no Aphra Johnson. Culpepper's suggestion is probably based on the fact that he knew there were Johnsons in
Sturry" (23). Since Duffy's biography, scholars and biographers alike have
accepted this version of Behn's origins.

When skepticism did arise, it did so not over whether Aphra Behn was
Aphra Johnson or Aphra Amis, but whether the events, which detailed a bit
of Behn's early life as reported in Behn's novella *Oroonoko*, were factual.
Ernest Bernbaum challenged both the novella's and *The Memoirs*'s valid-
ity as evidence that Behn had traveled to Surinam and, as a consequence,
the lineage that she posits for herself (Bernbaum 1913). Though Bernbaum
is highly skeptical of the value of *The Memoirs* as factual, he does accept
the document's assertion that John Johnson was Behn's father. Bernbaum
was much more interested in calling into question the truth-claims put
forth by Behn in her novella than he was interested in solving the rid-

dle of her birth. Bernbaum's argument that Behn borrowed heavily from George Warren's *An Impartial Description of Surinam upon the Continent of Guiana in America* quickly generated a debate and the problematic issue of Behn's origins once more took center stage in the scholarly engagement with her writings and life.

In this century-long investigation into the life of Behn, one of the consistent links between the different scholarly perspectives has been the rhetoric of historical speculation. That is, whenever a scholar or critic embarks on a discussion of Behn's life, they perforce must use conditional phrases and language whenever they discuss Behn's genealogy and, to a great degree, the details of her non-professional adult life. Todd's *The Secret Life of Aphra Behn* is emblematic of this tendency; her commentary is replete with words or phrases such as "speculation," "probably," "might have been," "possible," "perhaps," "seems," "appears," "apparently," and "so forth" (Todd 1997). For example, in a discussion of the Emily Price who is a recipient of one of Behn's letters, Todd writes: "[Behn] did not like the fervour of her feeling for Hoyle, knowing what a drug obsessive love could become. Her safety valve, besides writing and humour, was, perhaps, emotional promiscuity" (189). According to Todd, "this she may have indulged with the pretty young Emily Price." We quickly learn that the biographer is uncertain as to the exact identity of Price, perhaps the daughter of an actor, Joseph Price, or "a Captain Warcup, circulator of scurrilous works, a man perhaps known to Behn through her copying activity" (190). While Todd notes that she has "used the words 'perhaps' and 'possibly' and kept to the subjunctive," she also admits that her rhetoric occasionally has "lapsed and left speculation in the declarative. Not everything here is 'true'; nor is it likely to be proven one way or the other" (6).

Part II

A cool fog settled over St Hilda's College. The intrepid scholars made their way into the college's Senior Common Room, where the object had resided since being gifted to the college. "It's kind of small, not exactly what I expected." The pair peered behind the frame; it was screwed on. Gently removing the painting from its place on the wall, giggling as they worked, the Behn scholars carefully turned the frame over and read the inscription. Smiling at each other, the pair returned the portrait to its resting place and left, leaving only invisible traces of their presence — the visit to be recorded at some future date by one of them. (For Julia Briggs)

"A Painting ought to change as you look at it, and as you think, talk, and write about it. The story it tells will never be more than the part of the stories you and others tell about it" (Berger 1994, 87). There are three extant, presumptive portraits of Aphra Behn: one attributed to Peter Lely, one to his student Mary Beale, and a third attributed to John Riley. There are two questions I immediately asked when I first viewed the portraits. The first question was why the inconsistency in representations if Behn sat for each of the portraits? My second question prompted the interrogation that is this book — how do these images definitively prove the author of *Oroonoko*, *The Black Lady*, *Abdelazer*, and *The Unfortunate Bride* was white and not white passing? What Berger cogently postulates in his observation is the performative aspects of sitting for a portrait:

> In terms of what we assume about the actual painting and posing process, the portrait gives us a selectively abstracted and idealized image of posing. It creates a referential illusion. What it pretends only to reflect and refer to is in fact something it constitutes. Thus it represents the three-way diachronic transaction between painter, sitter, and observer in a purely fictional field. This is the basic plot, scenario, or fiction of Early Modern portraiture, and I call it *the fiction of the pose*. (Berger 1994, 99 original emphasis)

Illusion. Fiction. Pose. The first two terms patently figure in Behn's self-representation as well as her construction of characters capable of disrupting the illusions and fictions of race, gender, and class.

Let's begin by looking at the portraiture that provides a visual validation of Aphra Behn's whiteness. Figure 1 is attributed to Peter Lely; Figure 2 is an engraving by John Riley; and Figure 3 is attributed to Mary Beale. Figure 2 has the most illusive history as it is considered a lost portrait and what remains is a 1716 drawing by Robert White which is based on Riley's engraving.

Figure 1. Aphra Behn, by Peter Lely (https://collections.britishart.yale.edu/catalog/tms:51853)
Figure 2. Aphra Behn, by John Riley (1646-1691) (https://belchetz-swenson.com/aphrabehn; https://commons.wikimedia.org/w/index.php?curid=18838021)
Figure 3. Aphra Behn, by Mary Beale (http://www.luminarium.org/eightlit/behn/; https://commons.wikimedia.org/w/index.php?curid=18837859)

At first glance, the portraits of Behn (for the sake of argument, let's assume they are actual evidentiary representations of her) fall squarely in the "she is a white woman" camp. None of the stereotypical physical traits that have come to be associated with Blackness in the early modern period are visible — the broad nose, thick lips, and dark brown skin color. On the contrary, all three images offer a spectrum of presumptive whiteness, including the straight nose, thin lips, and pale coloring. Additionally, two of the portraits clearly share some resemblance (Figures 1 and 2); while the third is markedly different in depicting a woman whose facial features include fuller cheeks, slightly more elegant clothing and a necklace, and a cascade of ringlets.

What links these figures is the fact that both Beale and Riley apparently were trained in Lely's studio, and thus all of the paintings reflect the influence of Lely's training. In other words, the paintings are highly stylized and reflect not the actual appearance of the sitter, but rather, as Berger suggests, the represented image "of the act of portrayal" (Berger 1994, 98). None of these women can be nor are represented as they *actually are* because the very medium of early modern representation (painting or engraving) has an understood notion of what "likeness" means at different historical moments. This is not to say that the image of Behn is not Behn but to suggest that how that likeness is constituted varies according to the extant theories of visual representation governing the moment of portraiture.

To illustrate this point, let us look at an example of white passing that proved successful. In 1848, William and Ellen Craft fled the horrors of enslavement through Ellen's performative white passing. Ellen's successful performance as a white male was aided by her white-presenting appearance.

Figure 4. Ellen Craft photograph, Courtesy Avery Research Center for African American History and Culture, College of Charleston, Charleston, SC.

Trained to read the surface, to "see" what is reflected, few viewers of the portraits would doubt the sitter's presumptive whiteness. More to the point of this book, even fewer would ask or wonder whether she is performatively white passing. Within the contours of white supremacy, the viewer would have no reason to challenge the veracity of the skin color, or to ponder whether the intertwined ideologies of race and skin colorism that inhere in white supremacist logic don't skew the mirror. Whiteness, within this logic, is WYSIWYG ("what you see is what you get"). Under those conditions, each of these representations of Behn would unquestioningly be read as white in Anglo-American culture — as long as her inherited Blackness remained invisible. It is also this subsequent realization, I would argue, that sustains the white passing subject's awareness of her Black lineage.

Joseph Roach has argued that, "while a great deal of the unspeakable violence instrumental to" the "creation of the culture of modernity" "may have been officially forgotten, circum-Atlantic memory retains its consequences, one of which is that the unspeakable cannot be rendered forever inexpressible; the most persistent mode of forgetting is memory imperfectly deferred" (Roach 1996, 4). Did mortality trigger the "deferred" memories that bring Behn again and again to the matter of race even as she struggled to forget? Perhaps, while sitting for her portrait(s), seeing the Blackness painted over once more, she comes to realize that the multiple stories of her lineage may not be evident in the painting(s) left behind. Perhaps, she understood that her familial and cultural memories would be forever lost if not told or endlessly deferred unless mirrored in some other way — in the birthplace of Oroonoko, in the story of a pregnant, unwed young woman, and in Moorea, the Black woman whose husband left her wealthy and a Lady. Or even in her name.

According to Behn's biographers, the name Aphra is fairly common in the Kent area. Duffy writes:

> There indeed are two more Mrs Aphra Bean(e)s among the Canterbury marriage licences whom [Anne Finch] could have had equally in mind. Bean in all its variant spellings is a fairly common name in Kent in the seventeenth century and Aphras are thick upon the ground, also with many variant spellings. These two were spelt

Afry and Alfery. Aphra, which is to us so exotic a name, seems to have been very popular roughly in what was the lathe of St Augustine and particularly along the banks of the Sour. It was spread through the whole social range. (Duffy 1977, 17)

The name "Aphra" is unusual, despite Duffy's attempt to make it appear a common English name. When we interrogate the name Aphra Behn, what we discover is quite interesting. The word "Aphra" (and its variant spellings) has its genesis in biblical history. In 1 Chronicles, 3.20, Ophrah is noted as the offspring of Meonothai; while in Micah 2.10, the word "Beth-leaphrah" appears in an interesting comment: "in Beth-leaphrah / roll yourselves in the dust" (New Revised Standard Version). In the first usage, Ophrah, the word signifies in Hebrew a young mountain goat or a young deer, and it is used for both masculine and feminine case. In the second usage, "Beth-leaphrah" refers to a place name and "aphrah" means dust.

The Arabic name for what we now know as Tunisia is Ifriqya, which was Latinized as Africa, I believe owes its etymology to Arabic's linguistic kinship to Hebrew. In other words, the prefix Afra (however it might be spelled) and Afri mark a specific geographical and, I would contend, ethnic identity. With respect to Behn, is it possible that it might equally be a variant on "ben" as it is presumed to be a variant on "Beane?" And if so, does this signal the possibility of a Jewish lineage? This question has been raised by Behn's biographers, only to be discounted in favor of a Dutch or (in Todd's view) German lineage. So much of what is known about the name Behn occurs in The Memoirs, a text that, in my view, should be viewed with the greatest skepticism. The answers, of course, elude us. We can only speculate whether what we are given is accurate, let alone true.

The Memoirs of Mrs. Aphra Behn is a narrative whose status as historical evidence should be viewed as no more or no less accurate than Behn's novella, Oroonoko — for, as all of Behn's biographers since this one have acknowledged, The Memoirs draw far too heavily upon Behn's novella. In fact, The Memoirs is constructed along the generic lines of a romance novella and it is this generic decision that undermines the text's authoritativeness. Perhaps, when The Black Lady, The Unfortunate Bride, Oroonoko, and The Memoirs are read as interlocking narratives, we can get closer to what Baum calls Aphra Behn's black body (Baum, 2011). In tandem with these texts, was there a decision to make Behn the white-pass-ing subject as a "deferred memory"? Aphra can also be spelled as "Afra" or "Aphrah." Did a young woman of African and, perhaps, Jewish lineage, choose Aphra and Behn because they would serve as constant reminders of an invisible lineage? Did she write *Oroonoko* as an attempt to resolve her own internal struggle over the "unspeakable violence" that engen-dered her? Did Behn deliberately assume the mantle of the white-passing subject and then, as she neared the end of her life and when the eco-nomic and cultural policing of the Black body was no longer significant to her survival, leave the written traces of her subjectivity? Inscriptions like a birthmark to bear witness to the lineage that her whiteness concealed?

Marginality, displacement, alienation, loss, desire, nostalgia — these are the tropes that usually define the literature of white passing. These are also the tropes of exile. María Rosa Menocal, speaking about poetic exile, writes,

> [the exile eventually] must finally face the harsh winter night when [she] knows, in that full solitude, that [she may] never again see the [place of her birth]. In that cold and darkness, the solitary voice asks what [she] will do about it. Among the thousands of differ-ent answers that have come with the morning, one singular and unexpected one [writing the autobiographical narrative] has been a powerful and charming defense, a form of resistance commonly taken for *retreat.* (Menocal 1994, 91–92, emphasis added)

Rarely perceived as a type of exile, white passing necessitates the same type of psychic dissociation that poets and novelists have described in their depictions of the exilic state. Persons who engage in color passing generally must sever all ties to the community of their birth, their families, and, most importantly, erase all social and cultural traces of a "pre-pass-ing" identity.

It is a rare occasion when critics and scholars of early modern English culture ask what happens to those children of miscegenation who weren't slaves. Perhaps it is time we start and, in doing so, we also might want to query whether or not it is anachronistic to infer that the white-passing subject is of real concern in early modern England. In the end, it is the "fair Clorinda" and the "handsome Black Phillipa" who gesture from their literary graves at the margins of Behn's deferred remembrance. It is this twined wraith who stands looking over the poet's shoulder, guiding her quill as Behn embeds the codes of intelligibility, the lines of her white passing. Like the Phils, Behn is the racialized subject whose body houses the contradictions of race, and whose own subjectivity can never be fully realized because she will always be neither Black nor white yet Black and white. And, always a subject existing in exile.

The time spent in Surinam, in Antwerp, and in those self-imposed exiles (retreat) into the English countryside all left their marks on Behn's writings; writing cannot suppress the exilic anxiety conjured by the loss of an originary community. What is not discarded (as passing literature demonstrably illustrates) are the "mnemonic traces" of connection, of kinship, of belonging, which form the basis of a desire to recreate if not the originary community itself at least a simulacrum. What these exiles discover is that the substitute can never stand in for the original. For the white-passing subject there is no easy return home.

I have no conclusive answers to the speculations that guide this chapter on Behn's racialized identity, or the racecraft that permeates all of the romance texts touched on. The only point I would insist upon, the only conviction I hold dearly, is that the illogic of white supremacy and its color-based racism should not seduce us into forgetting.

Epilogue

In 2018 under the pen name Elysabeth Grace I published my first romance novel, *Fate's Match*. As I wrote in the author's note, the romance story of the main characters, Amina and Michael, had its roots in a historical and troubling narrative about a Black African woman ("the negress Maria") and the Englishman Francis Drake (Hendricks 2018). The series, *Daughters of Saria*, is indebted to a range of early modern English literary texts (John Milton's *Paradise Lost*, Ligon's *History of Barbados*, Shakespeare's *Richard III*, and, of course, the historical accounts of Francis Drake's voyages). The series owes a greater debt to Heliodorus's early modern English translators and adaptors, Milton's Lucifer/Satan, and to Aphra Behn for inspiring my scholarly and writerly interest in the intersection of racism and the romance genre. As authors whose fictional texts lay bare the racecraft at work in early modern English culture, these writers not only aided and abetted English racism, anti-Blackness, and white supremacy, they also exposed its fractures.

Fate's Kiss, Book 2 of my *Daughters of Saria*, is set during the reign of Charles II, the world in which Behn lived. The Black female protagonist of *Fate's Kiss*, Anne Willoughby, is a shapeshifter who engages in white passing. She is fully aware of the performative nature of white passing and the dangers inherent in being caught out. Yet, just as *Forbidden*'s Rhine Fontaine used his wealth and "whiteness" to ameliorate the plight of newly-liberated Black peoples following the United States Civil War, Anne uses her ability to become white to liberate or protect others, especially those who are targeted by racism and racial capitalism. White-passing Anne not only positions her whiteness as a buffer against racism; she does not diminish who she is as a Black romance character. In essence, like Rhine, Anne makes a deliberate choice to disrupt white supremacist logic (albeit, because *Fate's Kiss* and all of the *Daughters of Saria* novels are paranormal romances, Anne's principal enemy is Satan and his rebellious co-conspirators).

Comparable to Clorinda, Anne is a warrior, although a supernatural one. She is an expert with swords and knives and uses them against her enemies. Where the two women differ is in awareness of their origins and the outcome of their romance relationship. Anne is fully aware of her African-born matrilineal ancestry *and* the somatic skin coloring her white passing conceals. For Anne, whiteness is flesh she puts on and takes off as if it were a gown, something to be worn to protect herself and the women who who make up the exclusive Holland's League brothel. Anne's concealed Blackness, however, is not the major conflict in *Fate's Kiss* that it is for Clorinda in *Godfrey of Bulloigne* and thus does not constitue an obstacle to an eventual happily ever after. Both Anne and the male protagonist, Gabriel, survive the violence that nearly costs them their lives and the novel ends conventionally and in line with Heliodorus's romance.

Similar to all romance fiction, from Heliodorus to Beverly Jenkins, my novels work within the parameters of the generic conventions of romance. The main protagonists overcome the obstacles that impede their the happily ever after, the villains face justice for their actions, and the storyline is recognizable as a romance. As an author of romance novels, I am part of a larger writing community (Romancelandia) very much shaped by limitations and possibilities that the romance genre has promised since its inception. The possibilites of the romance genre lie in its popularity and accessibility, and, despite the naysayers, romance novels have probably done more for universal literacy than the genres of poetry and drama. While storytelling is inherent in all genres of literary writing, the romance novel engages its readers not as adversaries, but as co-conspirators. What I mean by this statement is that readers do not have to "work" to grasp the stories, the themes, or the conflicts at play in romance fiction. There is meaning but one does not have to master Greek or Latin, prosody, or Aristotelian notions of tragedy to comprehend what is at work in a romance novel. This not to say there aren't expectations on the part of the author or reader. Rather, what exists is a consensual relationship between author and reader that mirrors the relationship between romance lovers. This is the gift the romance genre offers to its readership.

However, the romance genre has also been deeply imbricated in racial capitalism and white supremacy. As we witnessed with Fairfax/Tasso's reimagining of Heliodorus's *Aethieopica*, the female protagonist's Ethiopian genealogy, her Black parentage, is irreconcilable with her white-presenting body. *Godfrey of Bulloigne* is the racecraft that allows us to see the racism at work in early modern English romance fiction. Because the world-builing of *Godfrey of Bulloigne* is temporally, geographically, and culturally different from the world-building of *Aethieopica*, how whiteness, Blackness, and white presenting work in the early modern English text must align with the racism operative in English social, political, and economic parameters. The forms of enslavement and colonialism present in Heliodorus's world are not identical to those at work in seventeenth-century England.

Therefore, to read or see the implications of Clorinda's Ethiopian-ness and the necessity for her death, we must attend to the anti-Blackness that maps cultural discourse and representations of Africans in early modern English cultures. The interchangability of Black, Ethiopian, and Negro as signifers of an ideology of colorism makes it impossible for any character who wears one of these labels to escape the effects of racism. While I am not arguing there is a direct literary genealogy between all the romance texts I've discussed in this book, I do believe the racecraft that necessitated Clorinda's death also set into motion one of the most pernicious and long-lasting cultural ideas within white Anglo-American romance fiction — the idea that Black people and happily ever afters are incompatible, that trauma, not love, is the definitive representation of Black peoples' experiences (especially in the United States). This view, sadly, shaped many of the nineteenth- and early twentieth-century African American novels even when authors placed Black love at the center of their storytelling.

At the end of the twentieth century, a sea change occurred in the romance publishing industry and in the romance genre as a whole. Technology enabled marginalized voices to circumvent the strictures of a largely racist publishing industry and produce romance fiction not bound by racism, misogyny, sexism, ableism, and classism. Within traditional publishing spaces, Black writers such as Brenda Jackson, Beverly Jenkins, and Francis Ray created romance fiction that not only centered Black romance happily ever afters but offered characterizations not steeped in trauma. These authors produced representations that reflected the complexities of Black American communities rather than a monolithic narrative rooted in Black trauma in the aftermath of enslavement, Jim Crowism, and white supremacist violence. While traditional publishing has been slow to embrace Black romance not designed for white readership of a certain age, class, and sexuality (primarily heterosexual or "cis-het") locked into a model of representation codified in white supremacist logic about what makes a "perfect" romance relationship, non-traditional pubishing venues have supported the desires of romance authors and readers from a variety of marginalized communities.

Whether dealing with complex social issues such as white passing, economic class, sexuality, disability, interracial romances, and community, contemporary Black romance authors reject the naturalized conclusions about the inevitable failure of white-presenting Black protagonists such as Clorinda or the Phils to enjoy a happily ever after. Romance as a genre tends to resist absolutes except for the happily ever after. Importantly, it is the romance genre's flexibility as a literary form to accommodate whatever fictional premise or historically-based storyline an author wishes to create. Paradoxically, it is romance's flexibility that also permits the detection of a culture's racecraft. It is this watermark of racism, in all its variations, that permits a study like *Race and Romance: Coloring the Past* to exist.

Works Cited

Baum, Rob. 2011. "Aphra Behn's Black Body: Sex, Lies & Narrativity in *Oroonoko*." *Brno Studies in English* 37(2): 7–29. https://doi.org/10.5817/BSE2011-2-2

Berger, Harry Jr. 1994. "Fictions of the Pose: Facing the Gaze of Early Modern Portraiture." *Representations* 46: 87–120. https://doi.org/10.2307/2928780

Behn, Aphra. 1915. *The Works of Aphra Behn*. 7 vols. Ed. Montague Summers. Volume V. London: William Heinemann. Retrieved from Project Gutenberg [EBook #29854].

Bernbaum, Ernest. 1913. "Mrs.—Behn's Biography A Fiction." *PMLA* 28(3): 432–53. https://doi.org/10.1632/457030

Boesky, Amy. 1995. "Nation, Miscegenation: Membering Utopia in Henry Neville's *The Isle of Pines*." *Texas Studies in Literature and Language* 37(2): 165–84. http://www.jstor.org/stable/40755067

Boyd, Elizabeth Reid. 2017. "Trashy, Sexist, Downright Dangerous? In Defence of Romantic Fiction." *The Guardian*. February 13, 2017. Accessed April 16, 2018. https://www.theguardian.com/books/2017/feb/14/trashy-sexist-downright-dangerous-in-defence-of-romantic-fiction

Boyle, Robert. 1965. *Robert Boyle, The Works*. 6 vols. Edited by Thomas Birch. Hildesheim: Georg Oms. Originally published London: Nachdruck des Ausg., 1772.

Boyle, Roger. 1953. *Parthenissa, A Romance in Four Parts* (1655). Los Angeles: The Augustan Reprint Society. Originally published London: Printed for Humphrey Moseley, 1655.

Brakke, David. 2001. "Ethiopian Demons: Male Sexuality, the Black Skinned Other, and the Monastic Self." *Journal of the History of Sexuality* 10(3/4): 501–35.

Brownlee, Kevin, and Marina Scordilis Brownlee. 1985. *Romance: Generic Transformation from Chretien de Troyes to Cervantes*. Hanover, NH: University Press of New England.

Bruce, Susan, editor. 2009. *Three Early Modern Utopias: Thomas More*: Utopia / *Francis Bacon*: New Atlantis / *Henry Neville*: The Isle of Pines. Oxford: Oxford University Press.

Butler, Judith. 1988. "Performative Acts and Gender Constitution: An Essay in Phenomenolgy and Feminist Theory." *Theatre Journal* 40(4): 519–31.

———. 1993. *Gender Trouble: Feminism and the Subversion of Identity*. London: Routledge.

Callahan, Diane. 2020. "Literary vs. Genre Fiction." The Startup — Medium. June 30, 2020. Accessed January 1, 2021. https://medium.com/swlh/literary-vs-genre-fiction-9173e11e77df

Carew, Richard. 1594. *Godfrey of Bulloigne, or The Recoverie of Hierusalem: An Heroicall Poeme Written in Italian*. Richard Carew's translation of Torquato Tasso's *Gerusalemme Liberata*. London: Imprinted by Iohn Windet for Christopher Hunt of Exceter.

Crenshaw, Kimberlé Williams, Luke Charles Harris, Daniel Martinez HoSang, and George Lipsitz, editors. 2019. *Seeing Race Again: Countering Colorblindness across the Disciplines*. Oakland: University of California Press.

Crooke, Helkiah. 1651. *Mikrokosmographia: A Description of the Body of Man*. London: Printed by R.C. and are to be sold by John Clarke at the lower end of Cheapside entring into Mercers Chappell.

Cutter, Martha J. 2018. "Why Passing Is (Still) Not Passé after More Than 250 Years: Sources from the Past and Present." In *Neo-Passing: Performing Identity after Jim Crow*, edited by Mollie Godfrey and Vershawn Ashanti Young, 49–67.

Davis, Lennard J. 1996. *Factual Fictions: The Origins of the English Novel*. Philadelphia: University of Pennsylvania Press.

Dawkins, Marcia Alesan. 2012. *Clearly Invisible: Racial Passing and the Color of Cultural Identity*. Waco, TX: Baylor University Press.

de Scudery, Georges. 1952. *Ibrahim, or the Illustrious Bassa*. Translated by Henry Cogan. Los Angeles: The Augustan Reprint Society. Originally published London: Printed by J.R., 1674.

Delgado, Richard., and Jean Stefancic, editors. 1997. *Critical White Studies: Looking behind the Mirror*. Philadelphia, PA: Temple University Press.

Doody, Margaret Anne. 1996. *The True Story of the Novel*. New Brunswick, NJ: Rutgers University Press.

Duffy, Maureen. 1977. *The Passionate Shepherdess: Aphra Behn 1640-89*. London: Jonathan Cape.

Elam, Michele. 2018. "Afterword: Why Neo Now?" In *Neo-Passing: Performing Identity after Jim Crow*, edited by Mollie Godfrey and Vershawn Ashanti Young, 241–46.

Fairfax, Edward. 1981. *Godfrey of Bulloigne*. Edward Fairfax's translation of Torquato Tasso's *Gerusalemme Liberata*. Edited by Kathleen M. Lea and T.M. Gang. Oxford: Clarendon Press. Originally published London: A. Hatfield for J. Jaggard and M. Lownes, 1600.

Fields, Barbara J., and Karen E. Fields. 2014. *Racecraft: The Soul of Inequality in American Life*. New York: Verso.

Flood, Allison. 2017. "'Lazy and Sloppy': Historical Novelist Philippa Gregory's Bizarre take on Genre Writing." *The Guardian*. August 14, 2017. Accessed April 16, 2018. https://www.theguardian.com/books/booksblog/2017/aug/14/philippa-gregory-lazy-and-sloppy-genre-writing-pornography

Frye, Northrop. 1957. *Anatomy of Criticism: Four Essays*. Princeton, NJ: Princeton University Press.

Galer Smith, Sophia. 2019. "How Black Women Were Whitewashed by Art." BBC.com. January 16, 2019. Accessed January 5, 2021. https://www.bbc.com/culture/article/20190114-how-black-women-were-whitewashed-by-art

Gilroy, Paul, Sindre Bangstad, Tony Sandset, and Gard Ringen Hoibjerg. 2019. "A Diagnosis of Contemporary Forms of Racism, Race and Nationalism: A Conversation with Professor Paul Gilroy." *Cultural Studies* 33(2): 173–97. https://doi.org/10.1080/09502386.2018.1546334

Godfrey, Mollie, and Vershawn Ashanti Young, editors. 2018. *Neo-Passing: Performing Identity after Jim Crow*. Urbana: University of Illinois Press.

Goreau, Angeline. 1980. *Reconstructing Aphra: A Social Biography of Aphra Behn*. New York: Dial Press.

Gottlieb, Robert. 2017. "A Roundup of the Season's Romance Novels." *The New York Times*. September 26, 2017. Accessed April 16, 2018. https://www.nytimes.com/2017/09/26/books/review/macomber-steel-james-romance.html

Hakluyt, Richard. 1903. *The Principal Navigations, Voyages, Traffiques & Discoveries of the English Nation*. Edited by Walter Raleigh. Glasgow: James Maclehose & Sons. Originally published London: George Bishop, Ralph Newberie, and Robert Barker, 1600.

Hall, Kim F. 1995. *Things of Darkness: Economies of Race and Gender in Early Modern England*. Ithaca, NY: Cornell University Press.

Hall, Stuart. 2021. *Selected Writings on Race and Difference*. Edited by Paul Gilroy and Ruth Wilson Gilmore. Durham, NC: Duke University Press.

Hamilton, A.C. 1984. "Elizabethan Prose Fiction and Some Trends in Recent Criticism." *Renaissance Quarterly* 37(1): 21–33. https://doi.org/10.2307/2861994

Haraway, Donna J. 1996. *Modest_Witness@Second_Millenium.FemaleMan©_Meets_OncoMouse™: Feminism and Technoscience.* London: Routledge.

Hendricks, Margo. 1996. "'Obscured by Dreams': Race, Empire, and Shakespeare's *A Midsummer Night's Dream.*" *Shakespeare Quarterly* 47(1): 37–60. https://doi.org/10.2307/2871058

———. (Elysabeth Grace). 2018. *Fate's Match, Book 1 Daughters of Saria.* Las Vegas, NV: Midsommer Publishing.

———. (Elysabeth Grace). 2019. *Fate's Kiss, Book 2 Daughters of Saria.* Las Vegas, NV: Midsommer Publishing.

Heng, Geraldine. 2003. *Empire of Magic: Medieval Romance and the Politics of Cultural Fantasy.* New York: Columbia University Press.

Hobbs, Allyson. 2018. "Passing." In *Keywords for African American Studies.* Edited by Erica R. Edwards et al. New York: New York University Press.

Huet, Pierre Daniel. 1970. *The History of Romances, An Enquiry into Their Original; Instructions for Composing Them; An Account of the Most Eminent Authors; With Characters and Curious Observations of That Kind.* Translated by Stephen Lewis. In *Novel and Romance, 1700-1800: A Documentary Record.* Edited by Ioan Williams. New York: Barnes & Noble. Originally published London: Printed for J. Hooke, and T. Caldecott, 1715.

Jameson, Fredric. 1981. *The Political Unconscious: Narrative as a Socially Symbolic Act.* Ithaca, NY: Cornell University Press.

Jenkins, Beverly. 1994. *Night Song.* New York: Avon Books.

———. 1996. *Indigo.* New York: Avon Books.

———. 2016. *Forbidden.* New York: Avon Books.

Leo, Africanus. 1969. *A Geographical Historie of Africa.* New York: Da Capo Press. Originally published London: Printed by Georg. Bishop, 1600.

Leong, Nancy. 2013. "Racial Capitalism." *Harvard Law Review* 126(8): 2151–226. https://harvardlawreview.org/2013/06/racial-capitalism/

Link, Frederick M. 1968. *Aphra Behn.* New York: Twayne Publishers.

Lisle, William. 2011. *The Faire Æthiopian Dedicated to the King and Queene. By Their Maiesties Most Humble Subiect and Seruant, William L'isle.* William Lisle's translation of Heliodorus of Emesa's *Aethiopica.* Ann Arbor, MI: Text

Creation Partnership. http://name.umdl.umich.edu/A02903.0001.001. Originally published London: Printed by Iohn Hauiland, 1631.

Mahoney, Martha R. 1997. "The Social Construction of Whiteness". In *Critical White Studies: Looking behind the Mirror*, edited by Richard Delgado and Jean Stefancic, 330–33.

McGrath, Elizabeth. 1992. "The Black Andromeda." *Journal of the Warburg and Courtauld Institutes* 55(1): 1–18. https://doi.org/10.2307/751417

McKeon, Michael. 1987. *The Origins of the English Novel, 1600-1740.* Baltimore, MD: Johns Hopkins University Press.

Menocal, Maria Rosa. 1994. *Shards of Love: Exile and the Origins of the Lyric.* Durham, NC: Duke University Press.

Mentz, Steve. 2006. *Romance for Sale in Early Modern England: The Rise of Prose Fiction.* Burlington, VT: Ashgate.

Moody-Freeman, Julie. 2020. "Beverly Jenkins." *Black Romance Podcast.* August 2020. https://play.anghami.com/episode/103009511

Morgan, Jennifer L. 2018. "*Partus sequitur ventrem*: Law, Race, and Reproductin in Colonial Slavery." *Small Axe* 22(1): 1–17. https://doi.org/10.1215/07990537-4378888

Morrison, Toni. 1992. "Playing in the Dark: Whiteness and the Literary Imagination." In *Critical White Studies: Looking behind the Mirror*, edited by Richard Delgado and Jean Stefancic, 80–84.

Neville, Henry. 2009. "Henry Neville, *The Isle of Pines.*' In *Three Early Modern Utopias*, edited by Susan Bruce, 187–212. Oxford: Oxford University Press.

Orr, Leah. 2017. *Novel Ventures: Fiction and Print Culture in England, 1690–1730.* Charlottesville: University of Virginia Press.

Paré, Ambroise. 1678. *The Works of That Famous Chirurgeon Ambrose Parey.* Printed by Mary Clark, and are to be sold by John Clark, at Mercers Chappel at the Lower End of Cheapside, 1678. https://www.biodiversitylibrary.org/item/257992. Accessed January 2021.

———. 1982. *On Monsters and Marvels.* Translated and Introduction by Janis L. Pallister. Chicago: University of Chicago Press. Originally published Paris: 1573.

Parker, Patricia A. 1979. *Inescapable Romance: Studies in the Poetics of a Mode.* Princeton, NJ: Princeton University Press.

Pearson, Jacqueline. 1996. Slave Princes and Lady Monsters: Gender and Ethnic Difference in the Work of Aphra Behn. In *Aphra Behn Studies*, edited by Janet Todd, 219–34. Cambridge: Cambridge University Press.

———. 2004. "The Short Fiction (Excluding *Oroonoko*)." In *The Cambridge Companion to Aphra Behn*, edited by Derek Hughes and Janet Todd, 188–203. Cambridge, UK: Cambridge University Press. https://doi.org/10.1017/CCOL0521820197.012

Perkins, Judith. 1999. "An Ancient 'Passing' Novel: Heliodorus' Aithiopika." *Arethusa* 32(2): 197–214. https://doi.org/10.1353/are.1999.0010

Pliny, the Elder. 1938. *Natural History*. Translated by H. Rackham. Loeb Classical Library 330. Cambridge, MA: Harvard University Press. Originally published 77 CE.

Puttenham, George. 1968. *The Arte of English Poesie*. Menston, UK: The Scholar Press. Originally published London: Richard Field, 1589.

Quint, David. 1993. *Epic and Empire: Politics and Generic Form from Virgil to Milton*. Princeton, NJ: Princeton University Press.

Reardon, Bryan P., editor. 1989. *Collected Ancient Greek Novels*. Berkeley: University of California Press.

Rhu, Lawrence F. 1993. *The Genesis of Tasso's Narrative Theory: English Translations of the Early Poetics and a Comparative Study of Their Signficance*. Detroit, MI: Wayne State University Press.

Roach, Joseph. 1996. *Cities of the Dead: Circum-Atlantic Performance*. New York: Columbia University Press.

Robinson, Amy. 1994. "It Takes One to Know One: Passing and Communities of Common Interest." *Critical Inquiry* 20(4): 717–18. https://doi.org/10.1086/448734

Sackville-West, Vita. 1927. *Aphra Behn: The Incomparable Astrea*. London: G. Howe.

Saunders, Corrine, editor. 2004. *A Companion to Romance: From Classical to Contemporary*. Malden, MA: Blackwell Publishing.

Stockton, Will. 2017. *Members of His Body: Shakespeare, Paul, and a Theology of Nonmonogamy*. New York: Fordham University Press.

Tamaki, Jillian. 2017. "Philippa Gregory: By the Book." *New York Times*. August 10, 2017. Accessed April 16, 2018. https://www.nytimes.com/2017/08/10/books/review/philippa-gregory-by-the-book.html

Tasso, Torquato. 1973. *Discourses on the Heroic Poem.* Translated by Mariella Cav-
    alchini and Irene Samuel. Oxford: Clarendon Press. Originally published 1594.

Thomas, Julia, editor. 2001. *Reading Images.* London: Palgrave.

Todd, Janet. 1997. *The Secret Life of Aphra Behn.* New Brunswick, NJ: Rutgers Uni-
    versity Press.

Underdowne, Thomas. 1967. *An Æethiopian History written in Greek by
    Heliodorus.* Thomas Underdowne's translation of Heliodorus of Emesa's
    Aethiopica. Edited and Introduction by Charles Whibley. New York: AMS
    Press. Originally published London: 1587.

Veracini, Lorenzo. 2011. "Introducing Settler Colonial Studies." *Settler Colonial
    Studies* 1(1): 1–12. https://doi.org/10.1080/2201473X.2011.10648799

Weever, John. 1922. *Epigrammes in the Oldest Cut and Newest Fashion by John
    Weever, 1599.* Edited by R. B. MCKerrow. Stratford-upon-Avon: Shakespeare
    Head. Originally published London: Printed by V. S[ims] for Thomas Bushell,
    and are to be sold at his shop at the great north doore of Paules, 1599.

White, Hayden. 1978. *Tropics of Discourse: Essay in Cultural Criticism.* Baltimore,
    MD: Johns Hopkins University Press.

Woodcock, George. 1948. *The Incomparable Aphra.* London, T.V. Boardman.